SPITFIRE

LIST OF CONTENTS

C000302113

4   **Mike Lima 417**
Graham Trant looks at the history of Spitfire Mk IX ML417 based at Duxford with the *Fighter Collection*

7   **Airframe Assemblies**
The Isle of Wight is home to this remarkable facility. Graham Trant reports

11   **Have Toolbox - Will Travel**
Warbirds Worldwide catches Craig Charleston at home in the UK. An exclusive report from Graham Trant

14   **Hull Aero.**
In the windswept Norfolk fens Rod Hull is painstakingly building up TE566.

16   **Dick Melton Aviation**
Micheldever is the home of Dick Melton Aviation, purveyor of classic Spitfire rebuilds to better than new condition

18   **Historic Flying**
Paul Coggan visits Audley End, the home of Historic Flying and talks to the Directors about their ambitions for the future

26   **Microscan Engineering**
Paul Coggan talks to Martin Edwards and Glenn Richardson about their CNC engineering business, specialising in warbird parts production

30   **Warbirds of Great Britain**
No major written work on the Spitfire would be complete without coverage of the activities of the world's premier Spitfire collectors.

32   **Spitfire Comparison**
Jerry Billings compares the Rolls Royce powered Mk IX to the Packard Merlin equipped Mk XVI Spitfires

CONTINUED OVERLEAF

1

LIST OF CONTENTS (CONTINUED)

35 Living History - Flying MH434
Mark Hanna of The Old Flying Machine Company writes about flying the Spitfire Mk IX serial MH434 - a piece of living history.

37 Kiwi Sixteen
Michael Shreeve takes an in depth look at the history of TB863 and its rebuild by Dave Lees of The Fighter Collection

42 Kiwi Sixteen - The Sequel
Following TB863's delivery to New Zealand the aircraft was damaged in an accident. Ray Mulqueen details the hard work and dedication that went into returning the aircraft to the air.

49 The Blood Red Spitfire
Graham Trant examines the history and rebuild of Spitfire Mk XIV NH904, appropriately registered G-FIRE

61 A Spitfire in Aspen
Bill Greenwood flies his Spitfire Tr.9 regularly from its high altitude base at Aspen in Colorado. Bill outlines some of the basics you should take into consideration when operating the Spitfire

WARBIRDS TODAY SERIES

SPITFIRE

This is the first in a new series produced by Warbirds Worldwide. For full details of our range of publications and the organisation itself please write to: Warbirds Worldwide, Five White Hart Chambers, 16 White Hart Street, Mansfield, Notts NG18 1DG, England

SPITFIRE

INTRODUCTION

For some three years now every time we have attended an airshow with the Warbirds Worldwide and we have been constantly bombarded with requests to produce a special publication on the Spitfire. So this new series - which we have called Warbirds Today - starts off with a title on the most famous of British fighters, the Spitfire.

It is only now, with so much activity surrounding the type, that it has been possible to fill this volume with material on it. Never before has there been so many Spitfire aircraft on rebuild, and never to such high standards. The industry surrounding the rebuilding of the Spitfire is a very professional one and this has become very important in the maintenance of high rebuilding standards.

Many people have contributed to this volume and to all of them I am extremely grateful. Graham Trant in particular put in

many hours and burned up many miles visiting various projects and organisations in the UK. Mark Hanna (Warbirds Worldwide's Chief Pilot) also burned some midnight oil in the preparation of his story of flying MH434. The remarkable story of Tim Wallis's Spitfire XVI TB863 was told at very short notice by Ray Mulqueen and makes fascinating reading. The engineers at Historic Flying made me feel very welcome despite their heavy schedule and an impending move to new premises.

One thing I have learned during my time with Warbirds Worldwide is that engineers are very determined people. Thick skinned, intelligent, hardy individuals who are often hard to get close to. They are a special breed and I feel honoured to have been allowed to see their work. And yet they are generally given little credit by the average member of the public for the work theyare doing. Regretably many people still feel it is a

matter of kick the tyres and light the fires and off it goes without a hitch. I have seen a Spitfire rebuild put ten years on an engineers' age in less than three years. To those that have built several - and many of them are featured in this book - time seems to heal, or perhaps harden the resolve to do an even better job next time. One thing that facinates me is that all the workshops smell the same. They may look different but the aroma is identical from Duxford via Chino to Wanaka. So to all the engineers that have put in hours of hard work, and all the owners that expend time and hard earned cash to finance the projects, this book is dedicated. Long may the Spitfire grace the skies worldwide.

The latest Spitfire rebuild to fly is the rare Warbirds of Great Britain Spitfire Mk XVIII serial SM969/G-BRAF (Richard Paver Photograph)

Mike Lima 417

Built at Castle Bromwich against contract No. B981687/39, ML417 was delivered to No..6 Maintenance Unit (MU), RAF Brize Norton, on 28th April 1944 and passed to No.84 Group support unit on 30th May. It was assigned to No.443 (RCAF) Squadron on 2nd June at Ford, Sussex, where it was allocated code letters 2I-T.

The Squadron was in action on D-Day and by late June was actually based at St. Croix Sur-Mer in Normandy. 26th June saw Flt. Lt. W.A. Prest claim a Fw190 as damaged/probable over Rouen, and 3rd July saw a forced landing at St. Croix, 9 July saw flak damage over Falaise, repairs being carried out by the unit.

Four days later ML417, flown by Flt. Lt. Prest again claimed a Bf109 as damaged/probable over the Alencon area in Normandy. Flak damage was sustained Cat AC in the Caen area on 25th July and on 7th August FB Damage Cat. Ac was recorded, this being to the

Graham Trant examines the history of the Fighter Collection's Spitfire Mk IX serial ML417. Photography by *Thierry Thomassin* and *Michael Shreeve*

undercarriage, and repairs were carried out by No.410 Repair and Salvage Unit, 417 being returned to No.443 Squadron on 12th August. On 23rd August the Squadron was at Illioers L'Eveque and on 29th September 1944 F/O R.A. Hodgins claimed two Bf109s destroyed,the Squadron by this time being based at La Culot in Belgium. The action with the 109s caused some damage Cat Ac and the aircraft was back with 410 R&SU for repairs early in October.

On 5th October '417 was allocated to 126 Wing and issued to 442 Squadron. It remained with the Canadians for the rest of its operational career, transferring to

401 Squadron on 12th October 194 No. 442 Squadron on 8th March 194? No.441 on 5th April and then on to 44 yet again before joining 412 Sqn. an finally to 411 Sqn on 29th June 1945.

With the European war at an en ML417 was despatched to No. 29MU RAF High Ercall in Shropshire, in Augu: 1945 and was still stored there in the A Ministry Home Census of aircraft i March 1946. ML417 was sold to Vicke Armstrongs, South Marston, Wiltshire on 31st October 1946 and durin 1947/48 was converted to VS50 standard at Southampton, as a two sea trainer against an order from the India Air Force. This conversion, completed i October 1948, with new constructor numbers being applied - 6S730116 - o the fuselage firewall plate and 6S73518 on the cockpit plate. The aircraft was te flown as G-15-11 prior to delivery to th Indian Air Force, where upon arrival was allocated the serial number HS543.

Colour Captions Opposite: Thierry Thomassin photographed ML417 during a transit flight to France for the La Ferte Alais airshov in 1989, from the back of the Fighter Collection's B-25 Mitchell. The aircraft had just been repainted complete with the insignia which was copied from a genuine photograph of ML417 taken during the war.

Details of the aircraft's career in Indian service are unknown, until it appeared in a compound at the Indian Air Force Museum at Palam in 1967. It was acquired by Senator Norman E. Gaar in April 1971 and shipped from Bombay in December 1971 aboard the *SS Eleni EF*, arriving at Charleston, South Carolina, USA on 15th March 1972. The aircraft then went into storage in New Orleans, before the engine, Merlin 266 No. V332968, was shipped to Paul Szendroi for overhaul in Chicago. The airframe was despatched to Fort Collins, Colorado in November 1972 for restoration by Darrell Skurich although little work was carried out on the aircraft. ML417 was later acquired by Stephen Grey and freighted to the UK. A contractor undertook the rebuild and modified the aircraft to single seat configuration and the aircraft was registered as G-BJSG on 29th January 1981. ML417 emerged in near original Mk IX form apart from wing tanks, and first flew on 10th February 1984 at Booker.

Although the aircraft was originally painted in its D-Day markings coded 2I-T of 443 Sqn., ML417 has received many coats of paint over the last few years. It was adorned in brown/green camouflage markings for the television series *Piece of Cake*, and has more recently been seen wearing the colours again with fictitious codes for another series called *Forgotten Hero,* based on the book by Richard Hilary. In 1988/89 the aircraft underwent another major rebuild at the hands of the *Fighter Collection* engineers. ML417 is an essential part of the *Fighter Collection,* is flown regularly by their pilots and is seen all over Europe for display flying normally being immaculately demonstrated by Stephen Grey whose characteristic grin from the cockpit has captured the enthusiasm of all that witness it.

Top: ML417 in May 1990 wearing filming colours for the TV series Forgetten Hero Lower: July 1990, back in its primary paint scheme. Both by Mike Shreeve

AIRFRAME ASSEMBLIES

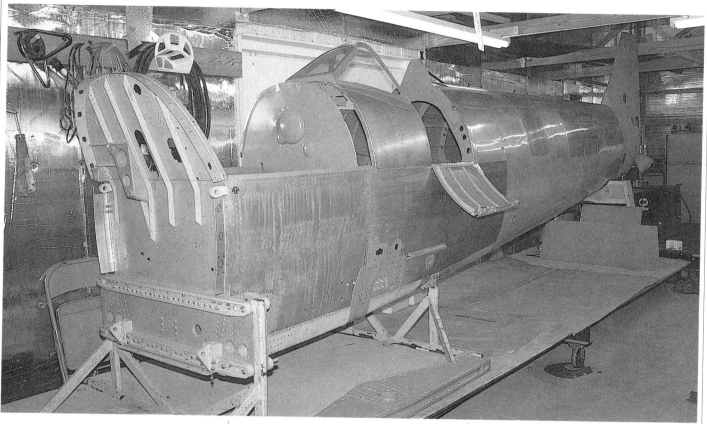

The vast growth in the warbird movement (particularly in Europe) over the past ten years has seen a number of specialist organisations formed to provide the required parts for rebuild projects.

While the US based organisations who specialise in the overhaul and rebuilding of both Rolls-Royce Merlin and Griffon engines are well known to *Warbirds Worldwide,* not to mention those who specialise in airframe parts for the Mustang, there are several workshops and engineering facilities here in the UK manufacturing warbird parts for the Spitfire, Hurricane, Tempest etc.

On a small industrial estate tucked away on the Isle of Wight, off the south coast of England one such company is located. *Airframe Assemblies Limited* founded and owned by Steve Vizard, a well known name on the warbird scene.

From humble beginnings *Airframe Assemblies* has grown both in size and reputation and is now able to supply all major sheet metal components required for use in a Spitfire rebuild. Steve Vizard's introduction to the warbird

world came through his interest in aviation archeology, in particular the Battle of Britain period, for living at Tonbridge in Kent it was in the skies above in darkest 1940 that the actual Battle was fought. Thus Steve was well placed to take part in many digs on known Battle of Britain sites of both RAF and Luftwaffe aircraft. Although outside the scope of this feature the aviation archaeology movement has assisted many rebuild projects over the years in the provision of parts for use as patterns for new build items.

Steve Vizard known in warbird circles for his depth of knowledge on various digs and the parts obtained, was soon helping various small museums and collectors with vital parts. The setting up, by Guy Black and Steve Atkins of *Aero Vintage* Limited at St. Leonards on sea in

---

Graham Trant visits the Isle of Wight, home of ***Airframe Assemblies,*** and talks to Steve Vizard and his team about the business.

One of the major tasks undertaken by Airframe Assemblies was the manufacture of this tail unit for Rudy Frasca's Spitfire Mk. XVIII (Paul Coggan Photograph)

Sussex provided the opportunity of turning a part time interest into a full time occupation and during his three years with the company Steve Vizard worked on a number of Spitfires including Tr9 PV202, Mark IXs TE566 and MJ730.

The early days of Spitfire rebuilding here in the UK saw most of the required parts being produced in house by the respective rebuilding companies. However, it was not long before Steve saw an opportunity to set up a specialist facility to manufacture various items. The opportunity of tapping into the sheet metal skills that existed on the Isle of Wight through a large pool of engineers who had worked with Westlands and Britten Norman at Bembridge (home of the BN Islander) was one which Steve quickly took up and soon the modest facility was able to produce such items as cowling sets for both Griffon and Merlin engined Spitfires.

Although initially based on his Kent home, *Airframe Assemblies* manufacturing work was carried out on the island with Steve spending much of his time touring the country, both seeking business, collecting raw materials and making delivery of completed items.

To date *Airframe Assemblies* have produced parts both large and small for a total of 22 Spitfire projects. In addition parts were manufactured for the Nick Grace ex Indian Air Force Tempests, Buchon and more recently Catalina, Hurricane and Hawker Hunter projects. From a modest start of being able to produce cowling sets, Steve was soon able to offer Spitfire rudders for all types from the Mark V rounded version right up to the broad chord Mark XIV style, elevators and ailerons soon followed, along with many other items of Spitfire sheet metal including undercarriage doors, radiator fairings and flaps etc.

At this time the warbird movement was starting to embark upon the major reconstruction (as a follow on from rebuilds) of the Spitfire. Again, *Airframe Assemblies* were well placed to be able to develop their skills into the production of all fuselage frames and longerons together with the many varied fittings that make up the Spitfire fuselage - in fact most items including the wheeled fuselage skins are available.

As a major supplier of components to the warbird rebuilding industry the world over, it was not long before Steve Vizard was asked to undertake the actual assembly of major components into sub-assemblies. Thus came their entry into the business of rebuilding Spitfire wings from the installation of new spars right up to the final reskinning of the complete item. The Isle of Wight workshops now include two Spitfire wing jigs and with planned expansion of their premises under way, *Airframe Assemblies* are well placed to be able to undertake more detailed work. The Spitfire wing is a complex structure with many thousands of components. Upon arrival at Airframe Assemblies wings requiring attention are jigged and stripped of skins. As each wing is in very different condition to the last or for that matter the next on the line, Steve's engineers never know quite what to expect or what they will find. Past discoveries include birds nests, bones and even dead snakes. Each component is removed in turn and examined/ tested as required in order to determine its suitability for inclusion in

the airworthy rebuild.

If in good condition a part will be cleaned, primed and then stored for future re-installation in the wing. However, more often than not a new part has to be made and here again the skill of *Airframe Assemblies* comes to the fore. Parts can either be manufactured using the old part as a pattern or from original Vickers Supermarine drawings.

The Royal Air Force Museum library hold many of the wartime Spitfire drawings produced by Vickers and their sub contractors although by far from a complete collection this valuable archive does provide one source of information.

The Spitfire, as originally built, had a somewhat limited range with its standard fuselage tankage, although in operations drop tanks of various capacities were

Jake Jacobs and Chris Michell of Airframe Assemblies working on a top longeron for a Spitfire. Airframe Assemblies have the capabilty to build almost any component for any warbird

used. In today's climate these would not be acceptable. Although a later series modification and installation of a rear fuselage tank behind the pilots seat was introduced this had effects on the aircrafts C of G and therefore proved undesirable. As most modern day Spitfire owners are looking to have a decent range capability for their aircraft on the

Spitfire fuselage frames awaiting delivery at the Isle of Wight workshops of Airframe Assemblies. (Graham Trant)

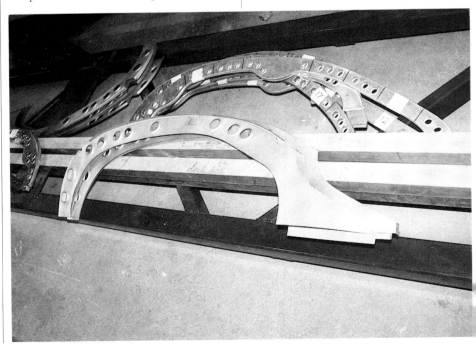

The busy workshops of Airframe Assemblies. Shown here are two wings being reskinned and refurbished by engineers at the Isle of Wight facility

airshow circuit, a number of wing types have been introduced, usually making use of the wing gun bays which are converted to take the necessary extra fuel tanks. Here again *Airframe Assemblies* have been able to fine tune their skills and produce the required items, both for their own wing rebuilds as well as for other projects.

Steve Vizard and his team are well pleased now that a not insignificant number of wings have been completed by them. The recent flight of Spitfire Tr.9 (from the BAE airfield at Dunsfold, Surrey) PV202 of Steve Atkins and Richard Parker saw one set take to the air, and the wings on *Myrick Aviation's* Spitfire, currently with *Trent Aero Engineering* at East Midlands Airport. This Spitfire, serial TE184 - a Mk. XVI, was for many years a gate guard at Royton in Lancashire following a period as a spares ship for the filming of *Battle of Britain* in 1967/68. It later joined a museum collection in Northern Ireland from where the late Nick Grace obtained it in exchange for the locally built Short Sealand flying boat; a far more appropriate exhibit fore the museum than the Spitfire!

The aircraft was soon moved to the mainland, where work had started for *Myrick Aviation,* when Nick Grace was killed in a car crash. The project moved

into the hands of *Trent Aero Engineering* with a first flight not too far away. After the wings of TE184 moved on to Castle Donnington, *Airframe Assemblies* undertook work as a sub-contractor for *RGC Aero Engineering* Limited of Sandown, on two Spitfires of the *Warbirds of Great Britain* Collection.

Steve Vizard and his colleagues worked on the ex South African Mark IX Spitfire BR601 as well as on the ex gate guard Mark XVI TE392. Work complete, these wings are now with *RGC* for assembly, ready to join the rest of their respective airframes.

The wing jigs of *Airframe Assemblies* now contain the wings of the ex Dutch Museum Spitfire PR XI, obtained by Nick Grace in exchange for a Mk XIV Spitfire. The Mk XI is now owned by Chris Horsley and is being rebuilt by the Medway Branch of the Royal Aeronautical Society at Rochester, with *Airframe Assemblies* under contract to strip and rebuild the wings, as well as to supply various other parts needed for the fuselage rebuild. As the PR Mk XI was designed to fly high and fast over long distances it had extra tanks built into the wings. These tanks formed part of the wing leading edge, which whilst under wartime conditions is perfectly acceptable, current regulations demand a more standard layout. So in the wings

being rebuilt at *Airframe Assemblies* the leading edge tanks have been deleted and the more desirable gun bay area tank modification incorporated - a complex process as the PR XI did not have any guns or gun bays! However, this is a minor problem to *Airframe Assemblies* and the work is now well under way. Whilst work continues on the PR. XI wings the team of skilled engineers are still turning out parts for various other Spitfire rebuild projects. In recent months parts have been completed and despatched to Canada, Australia, New Zealand and the United States as well as a steady flow of material for the numerous projects being undertaken in the UK.

Steve is assisted by his full time right-hand man Chris Michell, who, together with airframe fitters Dave Page, and John Miller and sheet metal specialists Hilton 'Jake' Jacobs and Norman Manby form the team on the Isle of Wight. In addition Steve has call upon the services of other part time fitters and a tool maker. With Steve on the road a lot of the time it falls to Chris Michell to spend most of his time at the Sandown facility working on the various projects, helped by the other specialists.

Now with 22 Spitfire projects having been supplied to date, *Airframe Assemblies* are well placed to continue in this specialist market. Aware that there is not an unlimited supply of Spitfires in need of rebuilding or reconstruction, Steve has recently taken on work building parts to support the Hawker Hunter in Air Force service as well as some for the RAF Museum's P-47 Thunderbolt project. The skills developed to satisfy the needs of Spitfire rebuilding are thus being applied to other warbird types. In fact Steve is quite clear that no warbird sheet metal work is beyond the capabilities of his company and some interesting projects are in the pipe-line, full details of which will be forthcoming through the pages of the

regular *Warbirds Worldwide* journal in due course.

While the standards of workmanship are very high indeed, all materials used have to comply with the exacting standards of the CAA and once completed have release notes or certificates of conformity issued. In fact *Airframe Assemblies* workshops are a regular port of call for the local CAA Inspectors when in the area. The workshops are festooned with jigs and part finished Spitfire components and while *WW* were visiting fuselage top-longerons were under manufacture as well as various components for the PR Mk XI wings.

Whilst the actual manufacture of parts takes time and considerable care it is also evident from the many jigs on the inventory that equal care in research, design and actual construction has been

taken here too, for once the jig or pattern has been produced *Airframe Assemblies* can manufacture any number of parts to the same specification.

Airframe Assemblies have not only worked on components and wings but a North American based Spitfire XVIII now sports one of their tail units. Steve has lost count of the number of wing tip sets they have manufactured.

With new wing spar extrusions now available from *British Alcan Extrusions* it is now possible to build wings from new. Here again Steve Vizard and his team have the knowledge, experience and skills to complete this complex task. For the future, 'new build' fuselages are not beyond the realms of possibility and **Steve Vizard is very willing to discuss any projects and ideas. Steve can be contacted on (0983) 404462 or by Fax on (0983) 402806.**

A mong the small dedicated band of airframe and powerplant engineers involved with the warbird scene both in the UK and the USA there are a few, who consider no task too daunting. Among these is Craig Charleston, who, over the past fifteen years or so has built up a good reputation amongst warbird owners as an engineer who has the skills and dedication to get the project completed to only the highest of standards. As one warbird owner was heard to remark at Reno '89 "If Craig can't fix it, then it just ain't broke!"

Craig Charleston started on the aviation scene as an apprentice with Rolls-Royce small engines division at Leavesden, near London. Having graduated he worked on many types of aircraft, engines and propellers, along the way obtaining his licences. This type of background proved to be a very good grounding for the warbird scene with which he has been more and more involved in recent years.

Although Craig had worked on a number of warbirds during his time at Leavesden it was not until an approach from the late Keith Wickenden that

Craig had a project he was to see right through from start to first flight. The Spitfire FR XIVe NH749 was one of a batch brought back from India by the Haydon-Baillie estate in 1978 and along with another airframe was purchased by Keith Wickenden. When found in 1977 by the late Ormond Haydon-Baillie it

Craig Charleston is well known worldwide for his skill and expertise in rebuilding warbirds. *Graham Trant* visited him at his Essex workshops

was engineless and propped up on bricks by the river Ganges. At the time of its arrival into the UK its RAF serial was unknown. However some deft work by Spitfire Historian Peter Arnold soon identified the airframe as being NH749, one of a batch of similar aircraft stored by the RAF in India, later being handed to the embryo Indian Air Force in December 1947. The aircrafts Indian Air Force service history is sketchy, but it was offered for sale in 1977 and later purchased, for importation to the UK in 1978. Craig started work on the aircraft

at a farm near to Hemel Hempstead in July 1979 and following much detailed construction work the aircraft was finally transported to Cranfield for final assembly, testing and first flight as G-MXIV. The Spitfire was offered for sale in Christie's 1983 Duxford auction but failed to reach its reserve and returned to Cranfield. The tragic death of owner Keith Wickenden, a Conservative Member of Parliament in an air crash at Shoreham, the Spitfire was again offered for sale.

Consequently an advertisement in *Trade-A-Plane* caught the eye of California based David Price who flew over to inspect and test fly the aircraft at Cranfield. A deal was completed in early 1985 and Craig was retained by Price to strip down the Spitfire and pack it for shipment to the United States of America. Having rebuilt the aircraft and packed it Craig needed little persuasion to go to Chino to complete the final assembly and supervise the testing prior to U.S. registration.

This contract was the start of a long association with David Price and his aircraft, for Craig has been called upon a number of times to work on the Spitfire

Have Tool Box - Will Travel

Engineer MIke Bloxham working on the installation of the cooling system in David Tallichet's Spitfire XVIII TP298 at Craig Chrleston's workshops (Graham Trant)

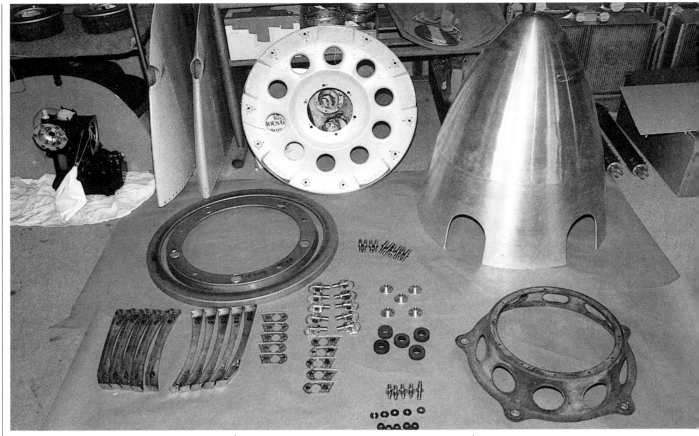

as well as other aircraft in the Price Collection such as the Sea Fury and Mustang etc.

The Charleston reputation for detailed, high quality workmanship and a high standard of finishing has been called upon by many warbird owners (usually, Craig adds, at short notice). When Spencer Flack's scarlet Spitfire G-FIRE had a propeller problem in Northern Ireland it was Craig who received the late night call for help. Soon packed into the back of an aircraft (complete with tools and a spare propeller) Craig was off to Newtonards to effect a propeller change, and allow the aircraft to keep its next airshow date. In fact over the years of the G-FIRE operation in other ownerships in the UK Craig has been called upon a number of times to deal with serviceability problems.

As time moved on Craig was also able to help with various Spitfire rebuild projects both here in Europe and in the United States. Among those to have benefited from his experience with the Spitfire, its Merlin and Griffon engine and propellers have been Bill Greenwood's two place Tr.9 TE308/N308WK) at Aspen, Colorado, the Mk. XVIII of Rudy Frasca at Champaign, Illinois and work·was also undertaken for the late Nick Grace on his two seat Tr.9 ML407 as well as on

the project of Peter Woods which involves rebuilding a Seafire 17 to airworthy status.

As well as being involved in the Spitfire projects Craig is also tied up with several other projects involving various Sea Furies and has organised the transportation of many other warbirds, successfully overcoming many problems associated with moving odd shaped objects! This however, is another story.

Having spent many years working at a number of different locations Craig looked around for suitable premises on which to locate his operation, and is currently based in Essex, just north of the garrison town of Colchester. The extensive storage facilities and purpose built workshops allow Craig and his engineer Mike Bloxham to work on the Spitfire FR XVIIIe TP298. The aircraft has been in David Tallichet's ownership since the late 1970s and although some work had been done on the aircraft at a number of locations in the USA, it was not until the aircraft arrived in the UK that work really started on its rebuild.

The Charleston workshops allow for the wings to be jigged, whilst reskinning work was carried out, to be followed by detailed attention to the fuselage. The project has progressed well with both Craig and Mike Bloxham working full time on the Spitfire. Mike worked for a

Faced with the lack of an airworthy spinner for the Spitfire XVIII project engineer Craig Charleston decided to manufacture from new. Total parts in the spinner are in excess of 400. (Graham Trant)

number of years with Monarch Airlines a Luton and has a wealth of experience o many different types ranging from Pipe Cubs to the Lockheed Tri-star .

At the time of the *Warbirds Worldwid* visit to the Essex workshops TP298 wa standing on its undercarriage and wor was in progress on the coolant pipe run: As with so many projects of this type it i the smaller detailed parts which take th time to either locate or manufacture Craig has been able to call upor organisations such as *Airframe Assemblie: Microscan Engineering, Cambridg Radiators* and *AJD Engineering* of Suffol for fuel tanks.Craig speaks very highly c the standards of work of his part suppliers but "even with so man specialists around there are parts you jus have to make yourself" says Craig.

As an example of this the five blad Griffon spinner assembly - something no given much consideration until yo realise that there are over 400 parts in i make up - is one assembly that Craig an Mike built themselves. TP298 did no have a good spinner; only the damage remains of one from a scrap yard was available . Not to be easily put off Craig decided that he and Mike would manufacture the missing item. In the event, they built a number and have some as stock. Craig was able to borrow an existing spinner assembly for use as a pattern and from this all the necessary parts were made, all to a high standard. This project is typical of Charleston's approach and attention to detail is one of his hallmarks. The current project is due to be returned to the United States for final assembly later this year when it will be mated with a US rebuilt Griffon engine and a propeller from Germany. The Tallichet museum in California have decided that the Spitfire will wear 152 Squadron SEAC markings when completed and flying again early next year.

For a talented team such as Craig Charleston and Mike Bloxham there is a waiting list of projects in line, although at this stage Craig is not saying which one will follow the current Spitfire. However, when it does take shape in the Essex workshops one thing is certain and that is that the very high standards of workmanship shown to date will continue to be upheld over the coming years.

As well as travelling the world on numerous assignments, tools at the ready, and having worked on a number of

Spitfire XVIII TP298, a temporary import to theUK is due to be shipped to California later this year (G.Trant)

warbirds, Craig has been able to build up a good stock of Spitfire and Seafire parts and Sea Fury spares, for in between spells of working on the projects he is a regular visitor to many surplus depots and even aircraft scrap yards. Not only is he well placed to rebuild complete aircraft, but is able to assist others as well.

A very long term project is the rebuild of a Seafire F.46 rescued a number of years previously from a scrap yard. Currently stored, it will no doubt

emerge at a later date having undergone the Charleston treatment and be well set up for an airworthy career. However, this will not be for many years to come as Craig has a waiting list of aircraft to work through first, not to mention his own Sea Fury project.

For parts, help and advice or restoratations Craig Charleston can be contacted on: 0206 -271485 or Fax 0206-272805.

In the flat windswept part of Norfolk where winters gales blow hard across the landscape lies the Broadland area famous in summertime for the Norfolk Broads. But in those dark days of the last war, this part of Eastern England was thick with airfields, many of them bases for the USAAF's Mighty Eighth Air Force. Times have changed with many a base having peacetime use in farming. Some however remain active with the Royal Air Force, such as Coltishall, and the USAF with Sculthorpe. Even Hethel, once the

Graham Trant visits Ralph Hull at Ludham in Norfolk to see the progress on several Spitfire airframes and view this exciting restoration facility

from the bright light outside the only remaining blister hangar a weather worn notice announces the presence of *Hull Aero*. To the casual visitor this is just

Mitchells' designs.

Ralph Hull hails from Belfast i Northern Ireland, and started his aviatio career in the British Army, or to be mor precise the Army Air Corps where (whils serving with the Royal Electrical an Mechanical Engineers) he graduated as a airframe and engines technician on suc aircraft as the de Havilland Beaver, Aust AOP 9, Bell-47 Souix helicopter, not mention the Westland Scout an Saunders Roe Skeeter helicopters; all fron line British Army aircraft. When th supply of Spitfires dries up Ralph will b

home of the 320th Bomb Group is active as a company airfield and test track for the renowned *Lotus Cars Limited*. A few miles to the North lies Ludham, seemingly another disused wartime airfield, where once Spitfires of the RAF and Seafires of the Royal Navy's *HMS Flycatcher* flew from. Here agriculture is evident with cornfields between the old taxiways and cracked concrete runways, and the inevitable manure heap so favoured by farmers in this part of the world.

A dead airfield, never again to echo to the roar of a Rolls-Royce Merlin? Yes, on passing, this may seem to be the case. But a small windsock stands erect in the high wind and all is not quite as it would seem at Ludham. For here on a small private strip are a handful of Cessna, Piper and even a microlight aircraft. Away

another general aviation company looking after modern aircraft. However, tucked away in the hangar depths is the unmistakable shape of a Spitfire! Could that be a second? A third? Yes, three Spitfires, for this is the home of Ralph Hull, proprietor of *Hull Aero*, and a man who has a long history of working on and rebuilding the most famous of R.J.

HULL AERO

Spitfire 14/18 hybrid HS649, now in th Dutch Overloon Museum as 'NH649' i 322 Squadron markings as 3W-f. Hul Aero converted this aircraft to a hig back Mk. XIV. Seen here is the hig quality restoration work undertaken b Hull Aero. *(Graham Trant)*

well placed to turn his attention to thes types, but that is another story for th future.

With some six years of Army servic behind him, Ralph turned to civilian lit and by this time the troubles in Norther Ireland had started to flare up. So after short period in 1969 working at th RAF's 23rd MU at RAF Aldergrov Belfast's International airport (where th major activity was the overhaul of th RAF's Canberra bombers)Ralph felt tha perhaps Belfast was not perhaps the be: location.

Marriage brought Ralph to the mainland and RAF Coltishall in Norfolk, just a few miles from his current location at Ludham. At this time Coltishall was the home of many of the RAF's Lightnings and Ralph found ready work for the British Aircraft Corporation as part of the Manufacturer's support team. In 1974, just over a year after starting work on the Lightnings, the itch to travel hit Ralph again - something he contracted in the Army, with its ever changing postings to new units.

The wide open spaces of Canada are very different from Norfolk and Ralph soon found work with Rolls-Royce Aero Engine Division of Montreal. 1976 saw a move to *Glenelm Aviation* in Westville, Nova Scotia, where Ralph ran the sheet metal shop for this general aviation company. After five years with *Canadian Pacific Airlines* where Ralph worked on Boeing 747, DC-10 and DC-8 series airliners (obtaining his airframe and engine licences), the lure to move on took hold once more, with Ralph, his wife

TE 566, the Mk IX Spitfire currently being completed by Hull Aero seen here in its early days at Ludham whilst fuselage skinning was underway

Laura and young daughter heading back to England.

Ralph Hull, owner of Hull Aero with their current Spitfire project, the ex Israeli Spitfire IX TE566, rescued from a kibbutz in 1976 and now registered G-BLCK. Hull Aero hope to have this aircraft completed early in 1991.

Continued on P39

Near to the historic city of Winchester, and deep in the rolling Hampshire countryside can be found the hangar and workshops of *Dick Melton Aviation*, a company founded just one year ago in July 1989 by proprietor and sole owner Dick Melton.

Although only a year since Dick launched the company he has been involved with warbirds - mainly Spitfires, and Merlins and Griffons, for more years than he cares to remember. To many he is Mr. Spitfire and one who so many rebuilders refer to for help and advice on their projects.

How Dick came to be in his spacious and well equipped premises, as with so many things, came from a chance meeting and the question "How would you like to build me up a Spitfire" the late Charles Church having bought Spitfire IX TE517 was looking for an experienced engineer to complete the rebuild, following a visit to the Hampshire Estate of Charles Church Dick Melton agreed to take on the project becoming Chief Engineer to *Charles Church (Spitfires) Limited*, a position he still holds to this day.

On 1st July 1989 the tragic death of Charles Church in Spitfire V G-MKVC came just as Dick Melton was setting up his own company. At that time many people believed the two events were connected, but it was a very unhappy coincidence of timings, as Dick and Charles Church had been working toward *Dick Melton Aviation* for many months prior to the accident.

Dick Melton Aviation are contractors to Charles Church Aviation for the operation of their airworthy aircraft as well as the rebuilding of a number of Spitfires obtained by Charles Church over the last few years. The death of the founder and

driving force was a savage blow, but now, twelve months on, work is progressing well and with the backing and enthusiasm of Susanna Church the collection of aircraft built up by Charles Church continues with many airshows and films to their recent credit.

Dick Melton Aviation is the home of **Charles Church (Spitfires) Limited** and is host to a number of exciting projects. *Graham Trant* reports from Micheldever

---

Dick Melton's interest in Spitfires started not long after he joined the Royal Air Force as an apprentice at Halton, for as part of that famous establishments training fleet was a Mk. XVI, serial RW386, which is now part of the *Warbirds of Great Britain* collection as G-BXVI. In later years Dick was to survey this very aircraft as a possible candidate for the *Battle of Britain Memorial Flight*, but at that time the RAF was not keen on Spitfires flying on American overhauled engines, so RW386 stayed on the ground. In Dick's opinion this was, at the time, one of the best of the RAF's exhibition aircraft having been kept in heated hangars for most of its life.

Following graduation from Halton Dick joined RAF Transport Command working from Lyneham on Handley Page Hastings and Bristol Britannias. overseas postings to El Adem (Libya) and Kormaksar (Aden) followed as a mobile engineer servicing the RAF's transport fleet on the trunk routes to the Far East 1962 saw Dick posted to RAF Chivenor in Devon to work on Hawker Hunters Not too far away was Exeter where civilian company operated the last RAF Mosquitos on target towing duties. With his vast piston engined experience Dic

Dick Melton Aviation

Spitfire FR XIV MV262 being rebuilt in the Hampshire workshops of Dick Melton Aviation for Charles Church Spitfires Limited (Graham Trant)

was soon called upon to help in the preparation of these last Mosquitos for their role in the filming of *633 Squadron*, filming of which took place from RAF Bovingdon to the North West of London.

During his time at Chivenor Dick became involved with the Spitfires of the *Historic Flight*, as it was then known, when he worked on a major overhaul of their PR 19 PM631 at Coltishall; the seeds were then sown with Dick having decided that a posting to the flight was a must for some time later in his RAF career.

As Dick was a Transport Aircraft Servicing Specialist (known in the trade as a Tass Man) he was soon posted away from the Hunters of Devon and Spitfires of the historic flight with a two and a half year stint in Singapore based at both Tengah and Changi working on VC-10s and C-130s as well as the Belfasts, Andovers and Comet 4s of Transport Command as they staged through on trooping and supply flights. His posting to Singapore also brought Dick into contact with the aircraft of the U.S. Forces as well as those of the Australians, Malaysian, Indian and other foreign air arm aircraft.

A UK posting soon followed with a period at RAF St. Mawgan, home to a squadron of Avro Shackletons, and more

work for Dick on Rolls-Royce Griffon engines, this being a prelude to his final RAF posting and the RAF's *Battle of Britain Memorial Flight* at Coltishall in Norfolk.

The BBMF of the early 1970's was very much a part time operation with ground and aircrews working in their so called spare time, it only being in recent years that the flight has grown in established strength to what many refer to as Squadron status.

When Dick joined the 'Flight at Coltishall he took on two Spitfire 19s, PS853 and PM631, the former being unserviceable! The Mk V Spitfire, AB910 presented by Vickers in 1965 to the RAF and the historic Mark II P7350 (which

had been made airworthy for the *Battle of Britain* Film in 1968) although this too was unserviceable when Dick arrived.

The flight also had the sole Hurricane LF363 (a founder member of the Flight at Biggin Hill in 1957 - the second Hurricane PZ865 - *The Last of the Many*- was not presented to the RAF until March 1972). With two Griffon powered and three Merlin engine aircraft under his wing Dick was kept very busy and after many long hours of work the u/s aircraft were returned to the flight line, the Mk II Spitfire receiving an ex Balliol Merlin 35, and the Hurricane even flying for a spell with a Spitfire four bladed propeller!

Rescued from its intended position at Hendon and the RAF Museum, the RAF's sole surviving Lancaster PA474 was flown from Henlow to its intended base at RAF Waddington. Although at this stage the aircraft was not a part of the Memorial Flight, a very close association was formed between the grounds crews of the respective aircraft at Coltishall and Waddington. The association stays to this very day, for one of those working on the Lancaster then was Dick Richardson, now manager of the Church owned Popham airfield in Hampshire, and project manager on the Lancaster owned by *Charles Church Spitfires Limited*. With his many years of Merlin experience it was not long before Dick Melton was involved in the

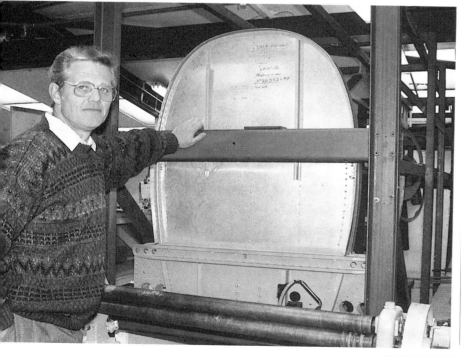

Dick Melton with fuselage jig in which a number of Spitfire fuselages have been built. The current occupant is a Type 509 Spitfire (Graham Trant)

CONTINUED ON PAGE 24

HISTORIC FLYING

When, in 1985, businessman Tim Routsis began negotiating with the Ministry of Defence for the release of several gate guard Spitfires, very few people realised that it would result, just five years later, in the formation of a company dedicated to restoring historic aircraft to flying condition. Not only has Tim succeeded in dealing with the Ministry of Defence (to mutual advantage) he has also brought together a pool of talent that will see many newly rebuilt but original historic aircraft rebuilt to a high standard and take to the air once more.

The Spitfire gate guard issue has been an emotive one, and one which many people, both inside and outside the warbird movement initially viewed with suspicion. The odd thing was that it was nothing new. *Warbirds of Great Britain* had made similar exchanges with the Ministry of Defence previously and this had involved Spitfire (RW386, TE356 and TE392) airframes. However, most real enthusiasts agreed that the Spitfires should be removed from the element torn positions on the gates of various RAF stations where, though for the most part they were lovingly maintained by

RAF personnel, they were starting to suffer as a result.

The contract negotiated by Tim involved four Spitfire XVIs and a rarer Mk V. RW382 was removed from its plinth at Uxbridge on 26th August 1988 and TD248 was taken from Sealand on October 14th the same year. This was

---

Paul Coggan visits the new home of **Historic Flying** at Audley End and talks to the Directors, Clive Denney, Tim Routsis and Ian Warren about the activities of this exciting new company.

---

later to go to Eddie Coventry of *BAC Windows*. The high backed Mk XVI TB252 was removed from RAF Bentley Priory on 9th November, and the rarer Mk. V, BM597, was removed from RAF Church Fenton on 26th May 1989, with the final Mk XVI, TE476 being recovered on November 15th 1989. The latter was subsequently sold to the *Weeks Air Museum in Florida*.

No doubt early involvement by two other talented individuals, Clive Denney

and Ian Warren has paid dividends. Clive founded and ran *Vintage Fabrics* for many years, providing a superb skilled service to many warbird and vintage aircraft operators. Ian Warren also had his own company and has a wide engineering based knowledge that has proven to be invaluable when rebuilding older aircraft like the Spitfire. Now all three are Directors of the new company, *Historic Flying*, and, as we go to press the company is set to move into impressive new premises located at the rural Audley End International airport in Cambridge, a most suitable location.

Though there are those that feel *Historic Flying* has yet to prove itself with the flight of their first Spitfire no one denies the work is of the highest standards anywhere in the world. Already *Historic Flying* have their first international customer as Spitfire Mk XVI RW382 is being rebuilt for a doyen of the warbird movement in the United States, Californian David Tallichet. David

---

Eddie Coventry's Mk XVI serial TD248 on the gate at RAF Sealand. This was the second of the gate guards to be removed by Historic Flying for restoration to flying condition (Phil Parish)

Left Hand Picture: RW382 in January 1989 just prior to work commencing on the main fuselage. The jig was very carefully constructed to the most precise standards. Even whilst work was going ahead on the first and second airframes at the Rayne workshops, plans were being made to secure the very rare Spitfire Mk V serial BM597 which was eventually secured from RAF Church Fenton in June the same year (Paul Coggan photographs)

has been continually impressed with the work carried out on the aircraft and hopes to leave it in the UK to be flown for the foreseeable future. Additionally, Eddie Coventry's Mk XVI TD248 is also well advanced, and will be the second Spitfire to fly with *Historic Flying*. No doubt the prize for *Historic Flying* in the gate guard deal with the Ministry of Defence is the Mk V BM597, and the Mk XVI TB252; both are likely to be retained for operation by the same organisation. There are plans to rebuild BM597 as a completely stock military airframe complete with guns et al.

So how is *Historic Flying* structured? Rather interestingly the company rebuilds Spitfires around an impressive system created by Tim Routsis and Ian Warren. Earlier this year Ian's engineering expertise and Tim's computer knowledge were pooled over an intensive three month period to create a document that details a rivet by rivet rebuild of the Spitfire. The document serves several purposes. It lists the physical tasks to be undertaken, time it is expected to take with the facility of actual time taken to be recorded. Effectively this means that any one of the engineers or Directors at Historic Flying can look at that document which can be adapted for use on any one Spitfire - and know exactly where the build is in terms of progress, ordering raw materials, manufacture of new or replacement components by outside contractors etc. It is this attention to detail, combined with the already high standards of rebuilding seen that stands

Historic Flying in good stead for the future.

Obviously, each of the Directors has an important part to play, and combined with the skill of the engineering staff this has put HF at the forefront of the warbird rebuilding industry. Ian Warren is responsible for general engineering supervision, metalwork and skins, whilst Clive Denney looks after fabric work and paint (it should be remembered that *Historic Flying* are not just rebuilding Spitfires but are looking to rebuild both warbird and vintage aircraft - many of the latter are fabric covered and this is where Clive's expertise comes in) and Tim Routis concentrates on general project management - an important factor in

keeping the projects moving and the business running smoothly. Tim also takes a hand in systems installation.

Work on the first Spitfire, RW382 commenced almost as soon as the aircraft was recovered from Uxbridge in August 1988. As we go to press the fuselage is complete and the Merlin engine had just arrived from Mike Nixon's *Vintage V-12s* in California. The wing jigs were painstakingly manufactured in May and the first wing has been totally stripped, new spars installed and is on its way back

The jigged fuselage of Mk XVI serial RW382 with work progressing apace. As soon as this aircraft was complete enough to be removed from the jig it was replaced by TD248. (Paul Coggan)

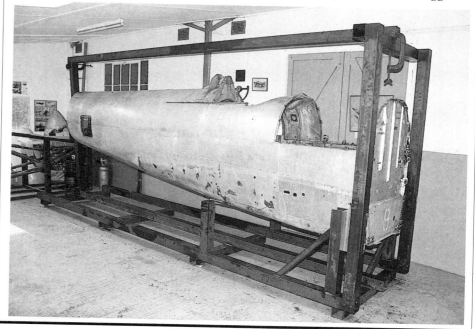

Colour captions overleaf: Mk V serial BM597 comes off the gate at Royal Air Force Church Fenton. By the time the last Spitfire was removed the Historic Flying team had the process down to a fine art and aircraft could easily be removed with no transport damage in just a single day (Top by Paul Coggan) Lower: RW382 awaiting engine alongside Eddie Coventry's low back XVI serial TD248 at the Rayne workshops (Paul Coggan)

Continued on Page 22

HISTORIC FLYING LIMITED

Audley End Airfield, Nr. Saffron Walden, Essex CB11 4JG.

We can rebuild your warbird or vintage aircraft to concours standards and customers specification at our specially built facility at Audley End near Saffron Walden in the United Kingdom. We have a team of experienced, skilled engineers and will undertake anything from a major rebuild to repairs. Metalwork and fabric work all undertaken to a high standard.

For immediate personal attention call *Historic Flying* on:
(0223) 314855
or Fax (0223) 68168

up. The move into the new premises is taking place as we go to print. Despite the pace of the rebuild no compromise is being made in the quality of work. The Directors of *Historic Flying* take an active part in the rebuilding process, to the point of hands on work. They are backed up by an experienced team of engineers including Kevin Bird, Linda Denney, Martin Hennocq, John Loweth, Laurie Tremble and Robert Turpin.

So where do you start to rebuild a Spitfire? The most astounding feature of a total Spitfire rebuild, and one that people remember most is the fact that every rivet has to be replaced due to the high magnesium content in the alloy rivets. The Spitfire was not designed to last into the 21st Century when it was originally

Top: Cockpit of TD248 just prior to work commencing on it. When complete it will look as good as the cockpit shown on Page 21. Lower: The fuselage of RW382 just one year after the picture on page 19 was taken and just prior to removal from the jig.

built.

The aircraft has to be dismantled to be transported and this includes removal of the wing bolts and hence the mainplanes. After installation in the fuselage jig, work commences with stripping out the entire fuselage; every component is carefully labelled, catalogued and cleaned for evaluation as to whether it can be used again or if a replacement has to be found or even manufactured from new. The *Historic Flying* system comes into its own here for it includes a reminder to order materials and parts at specific stages of

the project, and if outside contractors deliver on time the work schedules run smoothly. Tim Routsis believes that for every hour of engineering work undertaken he can spend three times as long chasing spares and components and so great emphasis is placed on project management at *Historic Flying*.

With fuselage stripping underway parts are paint stripped, bead blasted or cleaned, rectified (or replaced if beyond recovery) then plated or painted. The system makes notes on any specialist finishing required, and more importantly

avoidance of unsuitable finishing. An major skins that need reworking ar reworked or if a new skin is required it i remanufactured. As each piece of work i finished it is fastidiously recorded inspected and placed in store awaitin signature by the appropriate licence engineer. Of course with such a concis system in operation the Civil Aviatio Authority can trace batch numbers c paints and other materials and check tha all parts are made from the appropriat released items.

Work begins on the fuselage at frame

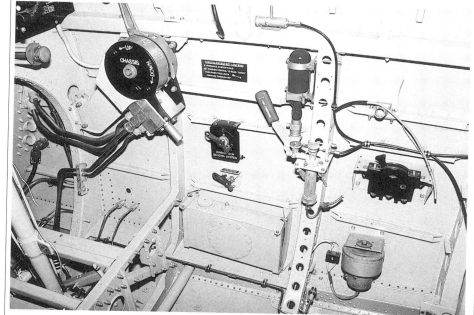

Another cockpit shot of RW382 in May 1990. Quite a contrast to the aircraft as it arrived here in late 1988 (Paul Coggan)

with the above principal being applied and the instruction 'paint strip/bead blast and inspect all parts - remake as required. Refit lower longerons'. Work then continues throughout the fuselage moving aft and includes such items as 'clean, inspect and anodise canopy rails, remake belly skins, inspect battery tray etc.' It is reassuring to know that even in an IT intense world some things never change - hence the instruction 'Polish instrument panel with boot polish' It looks good!

As well as the major fuselage items, systems are also built up in parallel and so the brake system, rudder controls, pedal assemblies, rudder bar and support structures are all ready for installation when the fuselage shell is complete. The control column is closely scrutinised, with all castings, forgings etc. being crack tested using dye penetrants.

The pilots seat is dismantled, cleaned etc. and the spring balance tubes reassembled using AGS steel taper pins. The armour plate is excluded, and new trim and harnesses fitted. Similarly the throttle quadrant is stripped, all the components paint stripped and/or bead blasted; all electrical components receive appropriate treatment/replacement as required.

The control cables are replaced with a new set of galvanised cables manufactured by The *Shuttleworth Collection*. All new canopy transparencies are made by an outside contractor and installed at the appropriate time. Fuel tanks are also the domain of an outside contractor.

At the same time the fuselage is being rebuilt the tail cone is also subject to a similar treatment. The tailcone is not usually removed to transport the aircraft and so this is done in the workshop after the rudder and elevators are removed. The tailcone unbolts at the fuselage break line. Ian Warren did the majority of work on the tail unit for RW382, but the next unit in line, that from Eddie Coventry's TD248 is being rebuilt in the jig by Kevin Bird. Martin Hennocq and Robert Turpin do the majority of skin remanufacture and these are made well in advance to ensure the other engineers are not stood waiting for these items and so rivetting the new skins on can take place swiftly and efficiently.

As we mentioned earlier fabric work is the domain of Clive Denney. Clive has done a large amount of fabric work under the previous company banner of *Vintage Fabrics* which Clive owned and ran with his wife Linda - *Vintage Fabrics* was effectively amalgamated into *Historic Flying*. This included work on the *Fighter Collection* Hurricane, Eddie Coventry's Yak 11 and countless Chipmunks, Cubs, and other fabric covered aircraft. The Spitfire rudder is next for attention. All the old fabric is removed, the trim tab de-riveted and the whole unit thoroughly inspected (rudders have also been rebuilt and refurbished for the Battle of Britain Memorial Flight's Spitfire Mk 19 PS853, David Tallichet's ex Indian AF airframe TP298 with Craig Charleston and the Mk XI of Chris Horsley, currently with the Medway Branch of the RAeS).

The wing jigs were manufactured in an intensive period of activity during two weeks in May 1990 and stripping of the first wing commenced at the end of the following month. As we went to press the new spars were installed in the jigs and the wings were being built back up. All internal parts had been refurbished or remanufactured as required and the wing skins are ready for installation. Obviously the wings contain several sub assemblies that can be worked upon including the

The skins are off! Clive Denney inspects the internal structure on RW382's wing installed in the jig. Since this photograph was taken the wing has been totally refurbished (Paul Coggan)

Continued on Page 29

G-CTIX/PT462, the first Charles Church Spitfire to fly after rebuild by Dick Melton, on its wheels in the workshops with systems installation taking place in late 1986. (Graham Trant)

Lancaster and by early 1974 PA474 was posted to Coltishall to join the BBMF. There was a public outcry in Lincolnshire at the loss of the Lancaster; not long afterwards the aircraft was christened *City of Lincoln*. In March 1976, due to operational reasons, the 'Flight was transferred to RAF Coningsby and PA474 came home again! By this time Dick Melton had completed his time in the RAF and with an Aircraft Maintenance Engineer's Licence obtained during his terminal leave, he returned to civilian life.

After over 20 years of RAF service Dick and his wife Carol planned to retire to Devon and run a small hotel with Dick saying "No more aircraft....never again..." However, move to Devon Dick did, but before long some short term work was required and he was working with *West Country Aviation* at Exeter in the fabric shop on Dakota elevators and rudders.

The lure of aircraft, engines and dope was too strong for the position of Deputy Chief Engineer with Shorts at West Malling in Kent was on offer and with his RAF experience of Chipmunks and Gipsy Major engines engines, Dick was soon hard at work on the contract Shorts had for overhauls on the RAF's Chipmunk fleet. However, Shorts did not manage to renew their contract with the RAF, leaving the future of West Malling in doubt. Dick was looking to the future again. By this time Dick had met with Doug Arnold, founder of *Warbirds of Great Britain Limited* who was in search of a Chief Engineer to take charge of his

growing number of warbirds, among which were many Spitfires.

Dick finally left Shorts and joined Fairoaks Aviation services as Chief Engineer and took up work in the newly erected hangars and workshops at Blackbushe, then recently purchased by Doug Arnold.

Dick Melton's main job was to work on the vast collection of Spitfires that Doug Arnold had built up and before long the workshops looked much like Castle Bromwich in its wartime days, with Spitfires soon to be seen in all directions. The Spitfire IX NH238 and Mk.XVIII SM969 were returned to airworthy condition, whilst Dick was at Blackbushe and a vast amount of work carried out on many other Spitfires including Mk. XIVs MV262, MV293, NH799 and Mk XVIII SM832.

It was not only Spitfires that Dick worked on, for the Arnold fleet included such types as the Mosquito (one of those that Dick had worked on at Exeter in 1963), several Ju52s from Spain, P-47, P-51, B-25, Lysander, T-6, Sea Fury and many ex Spanish Air Force Dakotas.

After some five and a half years and seven and a half Spitfires later Dick left Blackbushe to work as a freelance engineer for a year or so. At this time the late Nick Grace was working on his Spitfire Tr 9 ML407 at St. Merryn in Cornwall, not so very far from the vast RAF base at St. Mawgan, where many years previously Dick had been working on the Shackleton and its Griffon

engines. The Grace Spitfire project was progressing well and Dick was able to help with advice and practical assistance which resulted in the first running, in Spring 1985 of the Spitfires Merlin 25 engine. At this time Nick had also acquired the ex Strathallan Fairey Firefly AS6 WD833 and here Dick's Griffon skills came to the fore. A powerplant rebuild was called for and after incorporation of some Griffon 57 parts, the engine was run at St. Merryn by Dick and Nick Grace. This aircraft entered the Christie's Duxford sale of August 1984, being engine run on the morning of the sale. It is now owned by *Warbirds Worldwide* co-founder Butch Schroeder in Danville, Illinois.

It was around this time that the chance meeting with Charles Church took place and the offer to Dick to rebuild one Spitfire little did Dick know, when he agreed to take on the project, that it would involve seven Spitfires, or that it would bring him back into contact with aircraft he had worked on before at Blackbushe.

The first visit to the Church Hampshire Estate and 'the hangar' saw Dick confronted with little more than a clearing in the middle of a wood, a few tree stumps and no building! However, harles Church, with his building and construction group was not one to stand still for very long and soon the hangar and workshops were built to provide Dick and Charles with the space and facilities required to rebuild the first Spitfire, scheduled to be Mk. IX TE517, which was one of a number brought back from Israel by Robs Lamplough in the mid 1970s.

The fuselage of this Spitfire, a single seater, was quickly restored when, in mid 1984 and following much deliberation and discussion the idea of a two seater aircraft for type conversion came into being. At this time Robs Lamplough had just brought back the last of his Israeli Spitfires, a ten foot section of a Mk IX, T462 and this was to form the basis of a

John Lewis. The two seater Spitfire is now a regular performer at airshows and is available for type conversion of pilots on to type. It had been planned to follow the two seater with the Mk. IX TE517 into the production facility but plans changed with the opportunity for Charles Church to obtain Spitfire parts from both Holland and Australia and before much longer two new reconstructions were underway in the Melton workshops.

An ex Dutch Air Force Spitfire IX which had seen use for many years in a technical/school was located by Spitfire historian Harry van der 'Meer and was soon purchased by Charles Church. Over the years this aircraft had been robbed of many parts but there was at

aircraft had been acquired including a P-51 Mustang, a Hispano Buchon, Pilatus P-2, Fairey Battle, Lancaster and several other Spitfires. The Mustang (G-SUSY)Buchon (G-HUNN) and Pilatus (G-CJCI) along with Spitfire PT462 forms the basis of the Charles Church collection which is available for airshow and film work under the management of Dick Melton.

In the winter of 1988 Charles Church's thoughts were turning to establishment of his aviation interests as part of a different structure. Dick Melton had also been considering his future and after much discussion it was agreed that *Dick Melton Aviation* would be formed, based in the current workshops, firstly as major contractors to Charles Church to

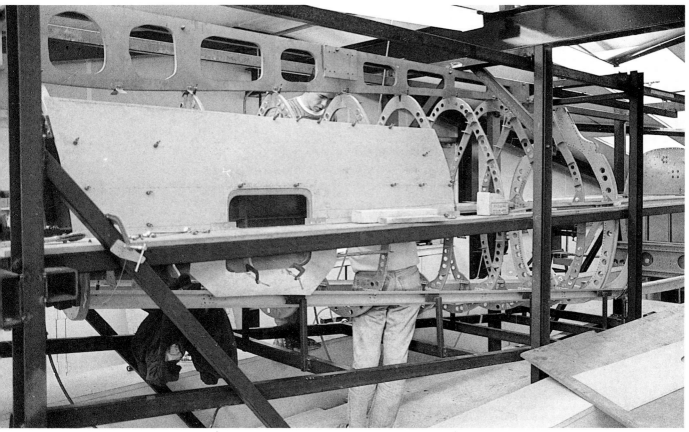

pe 509 conversion to full two seat configuration. The reconstruction of this aircraft and its subsequent conversion to full two-seat configuration called upon of Dick's skills, built up over the past thirty odd years and as the fuselage took shape in the jig at the Hampshire workshops the wings were constructed by Trent Aero Engineering at Castle Donnington. The tail section was constructed by *Air Repair* at Bicester in Oxon. Thus the first Melton/Church Spitfire was completed and later test flown from the Hampshire airfield by

least the basis from which Dick could start his reconstruction. This aircraft, with allocated serial PL344 is currently the next in line in the workshops and it is hoped the aircraft will fly before the year is out. As we go to press it was announced the aircraft would be included in the *Sotheby's* Battle of Britain day auction at Hendon on September 15th. The Spitfire parts obtained in Australia enabled Dick Melton to build Spitfire V G-MKVC in which Charles Church was to tragically lose his life in July 1989.

During all this activity several other

The famous Dick Melton Spitfire fuselage jig with ex Dutch Mark IX PL344, now G-IXCC under construction in November 1987 (Graham Trant)

rebuild and operate the Church collection of aircraft, while at the same time being able to take on work in its own right. Thus *Dick Melton Aviation* was born, only to be struck a cruel blow in its infancy with the death of Charles Church in G-MKVC.

However, Dick and Carol are a resilient couple and soon work was progressing

Continued on Page 46 25

MICROSCAN ENGINEERING

We'd like *Warbirds Worldwide* to share in our success - come on Paul, it's true so why not say it - after our first meeting in 1988 and your assurance we were certain to find a market for our services we have never looked back". And so began the interview for this article, to trace the success of *Microscan Engineering*.

Directors Martin Edwards and Glenn Richardson have one huge advantage in their favour. They enjoy the active involvement in producing the all important components for airworthy Spitfires - and other warbirds too. First they are engineers with the workforce and equipment to do the job. One owner told me recently " I go to *Microscan* and say can you make this part or this component. The fact that several other companies may have tried and failed is irrelevant. I know that if Martin or Glenn say it can be done it is an honest answer...".

Microscan have always been involved in the production of aviation related components from their inception in 1986. Parts for the Tornado and other modern aircraft and their associated electronic boxes have figured highly in the production at the Long Eaton facility where the CNC machines are constantly on the go.

The first Spitfire components produced by *Microscan* were elevator and rudder control levers for another contractor. The company now produce a multitude of Spitfire components for the majority of contractors in the Spitfire industry. Despite what some people will tell you

---

Paul Coggan visits Martin Edwards and Glenn Richardson at their Long Eaton facility near Nottingham and gets the facts on the manufacture of high quality Spitfire components

---

the whole commercial rebuilding side of warbirds is no longer a 'cottage industry'. It is a full blown, mainly professional industry with the same demands being placed upon it, (but perhaps more specialist) than other aerospace companies. *Microscan* have been quick to recognise the demands placed on it b the Spitfire industry in particular. Thou many people cannot get too excited abo piles of components the work produce by *Microscan* is almost a work of art, ar many rebuilders speak highly of the skills in creating much needed warbir components to exacting requirements.

A large number of wing componen have been produced so far and there a many orders coming in for componen from rebuilders like *Historic Flyin Warbirds of Great Britain*, and *Hull Aero* name just a few. Obviously fusela components are manufactured as well those for the wings. Orders are dealt wit on an individual basis but it helps, sa Martin, "...if people send in the pa number with an official order and exa requirements like number required, do it need anodising or crack testin, cadmium plating or other speci treatments'. *Microscan's* market is not ju restricted to the UK. Orders have bee coming in from the United States ar Australia too. Parts have bee manufactured for the Spitfire, Seafire ar Hurricane.

The most major components made

Microscan Engineering have made several components for the Fighter Collection. Fighter Collection Spitfire ML417 is one of a growing fleet of Spitfires that receives on-going attention to keep it airworthy (Mike Shreeve)

Continued on page 28

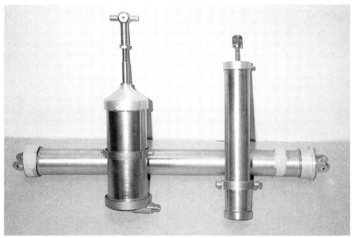 

Two very interesting shots showing the high quality of Microscan Engineerings products. The Left Hand picture shows the component parts of the flap return spring units. The top right hand shot depicts both original and newly machined flap ram units. "It is important that customers contact us at an early stage'....says Martin Edwards - 'for we can make parts from even the most corroded or damaged components'. (both photographs Microscan)

date have been centre spar booms (nine sets to date), undercarriage retraction rams (complete) and flap ram and return spring units. Undercarriage pintles have also been manufactured and there is a long list of customers for these items. *Microscan* are also called upon to finish wing spars from another source - a critical job indeed. As an example of the precise engineering required, if the main wing bolts are out of line by 020" the deviation would be 1 1/2 inches at the wing tip!

Microscan have produced many components and now have an impressive stock of drawings and specification sheets for many parts. They·have produced some 96 different components for one customer. Martin is keen to emphasise that advice on their ability to manufacture items should be sought at an early stage. "it is surprising what we can do using even a badly corroded component as a pattern - so please seek our advice before rejecting out of hand the possibility of us manufacturing a replacement." However, if you are submitting a drawing, suggests Glenn Richardson "please make sure the drawings are accurate - we have had the occasional customer say a part does not fit, and there is little we can do about this when components are made to our customers own drawings. We have some very accurate measuring equipment at *Microscan*, far more accurate than anything our customers are likely to possess. This is as a result of other products we have on the line...."

Of course many of *Microscan's* parts are now installed on airworthy aircraft and are proven to be reliable following longer term usage. No doubt they are providing a worthwhile service to the demanding Spitfire rebuilding industry across the world.

If you are interested in Microscan's **service you can talk directly to either Martin Edwards or Glen Richardson at Microscan Engineering on (0602) 736588 or fax your requirements direct on (0602) 461557.**

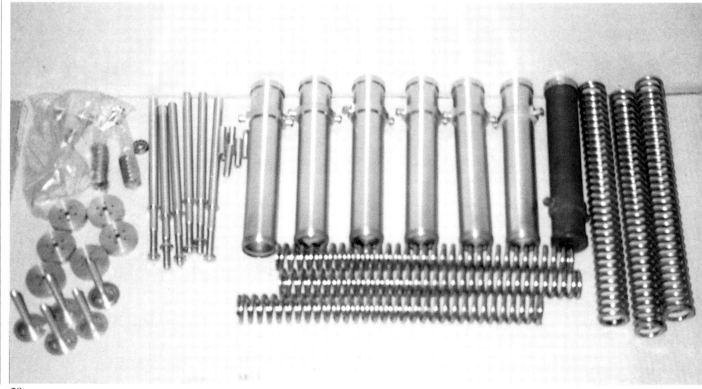

undercarriage main legs, wheels and tyres and the brake units etc. *GB Aerospace* provide new wheels and *Microscan Engineering* (one of *Historic Flying's* main suppliers) provided several new components including undercarriage pintles.

Meantime all the necessary materials and equipment for the radiators/coolant system, hydraulic system, vacuum system and pneumatic system have been ordered and the instrument panel is installed in the fuselage. As work on David Tallichet's RW382 is now well advanced, work is now well underway on Eddie Coventry's TD248 which is firmly installed in the fuselage jig. Therefore the second aircraft will undergo the same treatment as the first but, as every aircraft rebuild is slightly different (due to the condition of the airframe) this may be modified slightly. However the same system is being applied.

It is interesting to see that despite *Historic Flying's* lack of experience of rebuilding Spitfires engineering expertise has been used, coupled with Tim Routsis' management skills to create a system of rebuilding that is efficient and to a high standard. The very fact that the team had never rebuilt a Spitfire before seems to have actually helped them to perfect the rebuilding cycle for their first aircraft.

Once the first two Spitfires are complete *Historic Flying* have two more to complete. The high backed Mk XVI TB252 is in good condition and the Mk V BM597 is also complete. However, the company are looking to rebuild other types and negotiations are underway for other owners to house their Spitfires at the facility, for it should be remembered that this will be a maintenance facility in addition to the capability to fully rebuild aircraft.

As we said earlier *Historic Flying* are currently moving into a custom built hangar and workshops at Audley End, just one mile south west of Saffron Walden. The airfield is in a rural setting and the new 8000 square feet of hangarage is centrally heated and has a custom built spray bake facility, a new dope shop, an engineering area which houses lathes and other machinery, a self contained cleaning room, offices - from which an impressive overall view of the hangar is visible - and a large storage facility. It is located alongside a wooded area and car parking is available at the rear of the hangar, with a large apron at the front of the hangar, which will be fully operational by the end of August. The airfield at Audley End has an 880m x 30m grass strip (runway 18/36) and is ideally suited for the type of work being undertaken by *Historic Flying*.

For further information and advice you can contact *Historic Flying* at their registered office at 264 Newmarket Road, Cambridge CB5 8JR. Telephone (0223) 314855 or Fax (0223) 68168.

SPITFIRE

WARBIRDS TODAY

Audley End, May 1990. The new 8000 square feet of hangarage space is set in an impressive rural location just a mile away from Saffron Walden (Paul Coggan)

WARBIRDS OF GREAT BRITAIN

No major written work on the Spitfire would be complete without coverage of the activities of *Warbirds of Great Britain* and Douglas Arnold. Since the late '60s no one single warbird operator has been responsible for rescuing, recovering and having more Spitfires returned to airworthy condition than Douglas Arnold of *Warbirds of Great Britain*.

In many ways it was this organisation, and Doug Arnold in particular, that started the UK warbird movement. One of the first Spitfires to be owned by Warbirds of Great Britain was the very historic Spitfire XVI serial SL721. This particular aircraft is perhaps most famous as the personal mount of ACM Sir James Robb, RAF. It was taken on charge by the Metropolitan Communications Squadron in February 1948 and became the mount of Robb, taking up the codes JM-R. In December 1948 the aircraft was put on the charge of 31 Squadron, but still retained as Robb's personal aircraft. It was recoded JMR, with Sir James continuing to fly it until 1949. It then passed through a succession of civilian

owners until it was purchased by Douglas Arnold in early 1973, taking up the registration G-BAUP. It was later painted with the coded letters D-A. SL721 was later sold to Woodson K. Woods and is presently located at the *San Diego Aerospace Museum* in California.

Several Spitfires have been pulled out of India by *Warbirds of Great Britain*. These include Spitfire FR XIV serial MV262. This aircraft arrived in India in May 1945 and was assigned to ACSEA. However, just two years later the aircraft was sold to the fledgling Indian Air Force in December 1947. It was discovered by Doug Arnold in poor shape - basically a shell - at No. 1 Bengal Air Squadron of the National Cadet Corps at Calcutta and

---

Paul Coggan looks at the world's leading collectors of Spitfires Douglas and his son David Arnold, at the ***Warbirds of Great Britain*** facility at Biggin Hill in Kent

---

was shipped back to the UK. Later purchased by Stephen Grey the aircraft finally ended up with *Charles Church (Spitfires)Limited*. Spitfire MV293, also a Mk XIV, followed a similar route, and was used by the Indian Air Force as a training airframe, being allocated code T20. It was discovered at Bangalore and subsequently transported to the UK. It was subsequently registered G-BGHB and later purchased by *The Fighter Collection* at Duxford.

At the present time *Warbirds of Great Britain* have eight Spitfires 'on charge'. Spitfire Mk IXc serial NH238 is an ex Dutch Air Force Spitfire - it was issued to the Royal Netherlands Air Force on 30th May 1947 and carried the codes H-60, being taken on charge by 322 Squadron, being flown operationally against Indonesian terrorists. After being sold to the Belgian Air Force the aircraft was overhauled by Fokker and delivered

Belgium in March 1953. It made its [fir]st military flight as SM36 in May 1954. [Af]ter use as a target towing aircraft [N]H238 was acquired by a succession of [ci]vilian owners before being acquired by [Ed] Jurist of the famous *Vintage Car Store* [at] Nyack, New York in July 1969. Jurist [ha]s the aircraft trucked to Don Hull of [su]garland, Texas, who restored it to flying [co]ndition, registered N238V. It was later [pa]inted in the markings of Johnny [Jo]hnson. *Warbirds of Great Britain* [ac]quired the aircraft in late 1983 and it [wa]s registered G-MKIX.

[S]pitfire IX BR601 is currently being [re]built to airworthy status. This aircraft [ha]s a very interesting history having [se]rved with many Royal Air Force [sq]uadrons including 64 Squadron (July [19]42), 454 Squadron (Australian) - April [19]43, 129 (Mysore) Squadron at [Ho]rnchurch - July 1943, 316 (City of [W]arsaw)Polish Squadron - August 1943, [6]5 (Ceylon) Squadron -September [19]43. It later went to 3501 servicing unit [of] the 2nd TAF in February 1945 before [be]ing allocated for sale to the South [Af]rican Air Force. It arrived in South [Af]rica in March 1949, being taken on [str]ength with the SAAF as 5631. The [air]craft saw a succession of accidents at a

training unit before being allocated to ground instructional duties. It was later sold to Larry Barnett and came into the ownership of *Warbirds of Great Britain* in 1987 following successful bidding at a *Christies* auction.

The much rarer Spitfire PR XI serial PL983 has also lead a very interesting life. Currently in flyable condition after a rebuild (completed in 1984 by *Trent Aero Engineering* for the then current owner, the late Roland Fraissinet) and appropriately registered G-PRXI, PL983 is perhaps most famous for its service with the UK based U.S. Embassy Flight, being officially handed over to them in January 1948 with the American civil registration NC74138 assigned to it.

Several airframes are currently being rebuilt. The most recent airframe to take to the air following a period of storage during the move of the collection to the historic Fighter Command airfield at Biggin Hill is Spitfire XVIII serial SM969, now registered G-BRAF. This is currently the world's only airworthy Mk XVIII. It was recently re-assembled and flew for the first time from Biggin Hill at the end of July. Though it had an undistinguished service life it spent the majority of its time with the Indian Air

Force. Sold to India in in July 1949 the aircraft was serialled HS877. Later retired and kept at New Delhi the aircraft was discovered by Doug Arnold and shipped to the UK, later being registered as G-BRAF in late 1978.

Another rare aircraft currently being rebuilt is the Seafire LF IIIc serial PP972. The aircraft had a checkered history with the Fleet Air Arm, it having been in service with several FAA units including 809 Squadron, where it was coded D6-M. By May 1946 the aircraft had moved to Scotland and was based at Lossiemouth with 767 Squadron. The aircraft was one of 65 Seafire LFIIIc's delivered to France in the first six months of 1948. It was initially assigned to Flotille 1, later leaving for Saigon. It took part in early combat action in the Vietnam conflict in 1948. After some time in a French scrap yard Jean Frelaut managed to buy PP972 in 1970, moving it to the aerodrome at Vannes. *Warbirds of Great Britain* acquired the aircraft from Frelaut in 1988 and the basic rebuild of

Spitfire IX serial NH238 during the filming of Piece of Cake in basic camouflage colours, Duxford, July 1988 (Richard Paver Photograph)

Continued on Page 59

31

SPITFIRE COMPARISON

Flying the Spitfire IX

A sliding canopy with fixed rear view windows. When the canopy is opened it rolls back on rails, overlapping the rear view port and starboard windows. Opening is by manually pulling the canopy itself.

Cockpit

Port side has a throttle quadrant that is approximately 7 inches long, containing throttle, mixture, airscrew control and friction lever. The hood is closed by the normal left hand sliding back over the port shoulder.

Starting as per Pilots' Notes

Engine vibrations and general impressions: The Rolls-Royce engine is designed to run at high power settings and with start up, taxying etc. The engine appears to run rough and gives one the impression that spark plugs may be fouling. This changes once past plus four or rich mixture range. The engine then smooths out and runs in a harmonious low tone. Any misfire or fluctuation of its operation can be heard or felt immediately.

Controls

The flying controls on the Mk.IX (rudders and elevators) are covered with fabric and the normal acceptance of air pressure occur as compared to metal surfaces which are more sensitive. One will recall the terrific differences felt when metal ailerons were first installed on Spitfires. The approach to the stall is recognizable by the buffeting, just 10mph above the stall speed and makes the handling of the aircraft excellent at this critical airspeed or attitude. One can hold the aircraft in this buffet, in a steep turn and obtain a max rate turn at, or about the stall of following wing drop or flick manoeuvre- without worry.

Aerobatics

Aerobatics are easy and a pleasure with

Jerry Billing compares the high backed Rolls-Royce powered Mk IX Spitfire to the Packard Merlin powered Mk. XVI with the bubble canopy

Jerry Billing at the controls of Cli[Robertson's Spitfire Mk. IX (Robert [DeGroat)

the beautiful machine that it is. Inverte flight is not recommended for any lengt of time as the aircraft is not fitted with fuel injection system, but prolonge inverted flight for low level air display etc. may be obtained by precise an smooth application of the elevator contro in co-ordination with the retarding of th power control. This may also be execute by allowing the nose of the aircraft to fa ever so slightly towards the horizon at th same time. One other requirement is t have the fuel tanks 'full' prior to fligh Should the engine cut, no great problen arises; one simply recovers and throttl usage should be in keeping with engin handling, plus selection of either han wobble pump or electric boostpump (required). Loops and vertical rolls ar easy, keeping in mind the sensitive use the elevators. The elevators and rudde trims are powerful and greatly sensitive especially so at high speeds. Great rudde changes occur during aerobatics and wit power change and/or speeds. This mu be corrected by immediate and accurate use of rudder or rudder trim. Basically the aircraft is a pleasure to fly!

Mk XVI Comparison

At first glance one would view the Mk XVI as the Mk IX. However, the one piece bubble canopy is an identification feature of the Mk XVI (though there are high-backed XVIs). Otherwise all other features are similar.

Cockpit

The port side has a throttle quadrant half again as long as that in the Mk IX and is unnaturally designed at the low end of the power control. It appears to have been designed by a 'boffin' sitting at his desk simulating throttle usage whilst sitting back, reclining in a relaxed position, compared to a pilot in action who invariably sits more erect and slightly forward. Familiarity is quick in adapting to the Mk XVI quadrant - in other words it is too long. The one piece bubble type hood is closed by a crank gear in the starboard side of the cockpit and no locking device is required as long as the handle is released and engages the locking ratchet. There are no other great differences.

Starting as per pilot's notes

Engine vibrations and general impressions

The Packard Merlin has an entirely different gear ratio than the Rolls-Royce unit. This gearing may be recognised on start up and during taxying. When power is applied into the rich mixture range the gearing and its associated noise can be heard all the time. The Packard unit sounds much quieter on the ground than the Rolls-Royce unit but is blessed by a greater noise in the air! There is a definite contrast in the gearing mechanism.

Controls

The flying controls/elevators are metal covered giving a more pronounced and immediate response. Noticeable on take off and throughout the use of elevators. During the stall a very slight tail buffet is experienced before the stall occurs giving much less warning of an approaching stall; canopy and metal covered ailerons are all factors. If you are executing a steep turn the stall or dig in is simultaneous with buffeting; little or no warning is experienced. So you must not relax if you are executing a low level max rate steep turn. Recovery is, however, straight forward and quite easy.

Aerobatics

The Spitfire Mk XVI is also a pleasure to fly, but a slight difference exists compared to its counterpart the Mk IX. Because of the metal covered elevators it is much more sensitive and exact. Given a ten minute flight one becomes quickly accustomed to the increased response. During a vertical roll and recovery one should take note of this factor - as the stall without much buffeting will occur. Recovery is easy and straightforward - 100-120mph (from vertical). During inverted flight elevator response should also be remembered. No other variance occurs.

Stall

A vibration of the hood occurs in this aircraft and may be recognized similar to the tail buffeting on the Mk IX when approaching the stall. Obviously hood

Actor Cliff Robertson in front of MK923 with his crew at Oshkosh, 1st August 1987 (Robert DeGroat)

contour is responsible for this phenomenon.

Summary

In summary, tail buffeting is pronounced in the Mk IX, vice hood vibration on Mk XVI on approach to the stall. The metal controls elevator demand more attention in the Mk XVI. The gearing mechanism of the Mk XVI changes the tone as compared to the Rolls-Royce purr at high speeds or in flight. Ground tone is quieter on the Mk XVI than the Mk IX as described. Inverted flight for one minute or more duration is possible for low level aerobatics if executed as stated. The throttle quadrant, although slightly unorthodox can be easily overcome with practice on the Mk XVI.

This comparison is in keeping with current low level aerobatics executed during 1980 and 1982 on Cliff Robertson's Mk IX serial NR923 and Woodson K. Woods Mk XVI serial SL721.

FAA and DoT low level aerobatic proficiency ratings of - Manoeuvre Limitations; None and Altitude Limitations: None have been in effect for the writer, qualified on Spitfire and Bellanca Decathlon since July 1976 up to and including 30th April 1990. The writer has also been current on the Spitfire from early 1942 to date. A low level aerobatic proficiency rating on the Supermarine Spitfire is unique in itself and is the only one in North America. Several great pilots on Spitfires could hold this rating but opportunity is a prime requisite.

We are very fortunate to have amongst us two very keen air minded and easy to converse with chaps in Cliff Robertson and Woodson K. Woods. Without their keenness the public would not be able to view the graceful Spitfire.

The Spitfire, whether as the Mk I, II, VIII, IX or XVI is one of the easiest aircraft to fly that I have experienced. Landing is very simple and can be done without any great usage of controls. Brakes are rarely used at any time. Three point landings are a complete pleasure. It is recommended that the seat should be quite low to give a good view past the exhaust stacks. All marks of Spitfire are great for low level aerobatics. The Mk IX (elliptical)however proves to be excellent for a complete (within the confines of the aeroplane) low level airshow.

Maintenance

Crew Chief on Cliff Robertson's NR923, Erik Billing, takes up the story. The aeroplane is a joy to look after and really there is not much upkeep as long as all the systems are checked, and properly maintained. We have found that our biggest problem is finding nitrogen for brakes and flaps, although we have an on board compressor we like to keep our supply bottle at 2300lbs (which is located at the back of the aeroplane, forward of the accumulator hatch) in case we arrive at an airport that does not have nitrogen.

My father Jerry has been flying the Spitfire for the past 48 years. The only non-original item installed on Cliff Robertson's aeroplane is the emergency air replensihment bottle incorporated into the standard air bottles behind the seat with an open/close valve, in the cockpit to (if required) boost up the cockpit brake pressure if it begins to fall (so the pilot has brakes etc. on landing). The cockpit layout is identical to when the aircraft served with 126 Squadron on D-Day. The radios are located on both sides of the seat below eye level - the VOR head is the only change, being mounted to the left of the gunsight.

SPITFIRE

WARBIRDS TODAY

LIVING HISTORY

A vigorous head nod from Ray - "Power" 2650 RPM and the boosts coming up. Hand gesture left and we start to roll, sky becomes horizon then green meadows, houses. I'm in the number two slot, echelon starboard and concentrating on "hanging in there" - glued to and looking down leads' elevator hinge line and lining up his outer aileron bracket with the tip of his spinner. As I look through past his aeroplane there is Carl hanging on in echelon port. It's harder for him at the moment as beyond our Spitfires he has a face full of sky and bright sunshine. The speed is increasing and in my peripheral vision I'm aware that the ground is getting closer. I'm concious of holding a push force on the control column which is starting to make my flying ragged in pitch - hand rapidly off the throttle - trim, trim, back to the power. I've dropped back 2 or 3 feet and I need to sort out the rudder as well. It's trimmed for 220 knots and now we are making better than 290. Stop OVERCONTROLLING! I'm pouring sweat already and we haven't

Mark Hanna of *The Old Flying Machine Company* details the qualities of the very historical Spitfire Mk IX MH434, and tells of his experiences flying the type.

even started yet! Beginning to roll out now and I'm aware of trees, rushing green blur. Remember the brief. Do NOT sit plane low on the leader! Tighten it up, here comes the crowd line. Hold it, hold it, and over the airfield. Head nod from lead and one R/T transmission "power"- boost coming up +6, +8, +10 and we're pitching up, up and starting roll right. Nothing matters now but keeping station on the lead Spitfire - we're nearly on our backs, the controls are feeling sloppier and if I had the capacity I'd see the speed at 110 or so.

I'm still carrying a lot of power and it feels like I'm cross controlled. I have to keep working at that but now the noses are coming down, the power's coming back a bit, we've completed our wing over and can feel the controls coming good again as the speed increases. It's rough and bumpy. It's a hot day and the Spitfires are getting thumped and smashed around as us inside them! I'm saturated and my eyes are stinging as sweat is running into them - this next bit is my least favourite part of the display - it is the first loop on the 45 line. Out of the corner of my eye I am aware of the ground coming up and rushing by, head nod and pitch, pitch. There's a tendency to overcontrol on the Spitfire, the elevators are so light you have to work positively at relaxing all the time. Upside down on top of the loop slightly plane low on the leader pull - oops light buffet from the tail - the aeroplane saying don't pull any more! Jeez, this isn't just fun, it's hard work!

Mark Hanna taxying in the Old Flying Machine Company's Spitfire IX MH434 in one of the multitude of paint schemes worn by the aircraft in the last five years (Richard Paver)

To my eye the late Merlin engined Spitfires are the most beautiful World War II Fighters. In addition the aircraft exudes an air of history and nostalgia, particularly perhaps to me, a Briton! Our aeroplane, MH434 has to me a particular aura. This I think is because it has never been rebuilt and is largely original; it has been flying non-stop since August 1943. It also has a fantastic and impeccably documented history, having been flown by both a South African and a Belgian ace and having five 'kills' to its credit. It is so original, Stephen Grey says it has original oil in it!

On the ground the Spitfire is all curves and streamlines although the IX series have a pugnacious appearance in the nose area with the closely fitted cowlings providing impressive looking power bulges. On close examination, the Classic elliptical wing has a pronounced twist - 'washout' towards the tip, a very complex looking design. The undercarriage appears very delicate and the track on the wheels narrow. The propeller looks huge and the tail rather too small. If you mentally lift the tail into the take off position you realise that the four bladed Dowty Rotol prop is very close to the ground.

Entering the Spitfire is straightforward. The step up onto the left wing is easy. Depress the tiny push button on top of the hood and slide back the canopy. Then lean inside and open the small door on the left side. Once settled into the cockpit you are aware that the instrument layout has an untidy appearance although they are fairly logically grouped. There is no floor - beneath you are control runs and then below them the skin of the underside of the aeroplane.

The cockpit from left to right; Back and low beneath your elbow on MH434 is the master air cock for the pneumatic systems. Brakes, flaps, radiator shutters are all pneumatically operated in the Spitfire. This cock allows the valuable air to be stored between flights. Otherwise you are going to have a hard time taxying without brakes! Open the cock and you see air pressure immediately to the triple pressure gauge at 300psi. Further forwards we see the rudder trim knob. Wind this fully clockwise for full right rudder trim for take off. Next the elevator trim wheel. Free and full movement then I set it fully back (nose up) to help me hold the stick back when I come to the run up. Underneath the elevator trim

wheel are three electrical switches, pitot heat, camera master and the manual override for the automatic radiator. Beneath these is the 720 channel radio. Forwards and up we have the throttle quadrant combining throttle handle with radio transmit button on the end and the propeller RPM lever. The idle cut off/mixture lever on MH434 is inoperative and has been relocated on the lower left instrument panel. The throttle is gated at +6 boost (42") and it requires a positive rock outboard to get the +12 (54") available on our

aeroplane.

The instrument panel consists of the six standard flying instruments dead centre. To the left top we have our lights, pneumatic flap switch - up or down, oxygen panel, fuel tank air pressure gauge (used for transferring wing fuel to the main tanks) and the undercarriage up/down indicator lights. Beneath the main blind flying panel are cockpit light dimmers, starter and booster coil buttons and the main on/off cock for the fuel. Below that between your legs is the giant compass. Right hand side of the instrument panel is the important stuff; G meter, air suction, and a gaggle of engine instruments and fuel cocks. Big RPM gauge, boost (MP) radiator temperature gauge (most looked at item), with oil pressure and temperature in very close second place. Fuel gauge - activated by a pushbutton. Only the last 37 gallons are gauged of a total system of 135 gallons. Below the fuel gauge are several cocks utilised for transferring wing fuel to the main fuselage tanks (you cannot feed the engine direct from the wings and have to allow enough airspace (50 gallons) before transferring the wing

fuel. Also in this area is the huge brass kigass priming knob. On the right hand side of the cockpit wall mounted high is the wobble pump - this Spitfire has no electric fuel pump and you need to build pressure in the lines pre-start, using this.

Down by your right hand knee is the undercarriage control. Behind this is a rather inadequate looking undercarriage blow down bottle and lever and the go forward lever for the inertia reel of the shoulder harness. In front of you is the rather high control column with the famous spade grip. This is cleverly hinged about 1/2 way up for the aileron control and readily prevents the control restriction sometimes evident in roll caused by the control column coming hard up against knees and legs (P-51 and Me109). Also on the control column is the brake lever tied into the rudder. Rudder neutral and apply brake you'll receive equal pressure to each wheelbrake. Full right rudder or vice versa and you'll only get brake to that wheel.

That's the run round the cockpit. ready to start. The battery master is external - so power on. Air on, parking brake on the control column set on. Set the throttle to 1/2 inch open, fuel on, start and booster coil covers over the buttons down. Pull the idle cut off ring and wobble the wobble pump 30 times and watch the fuel pressure warning light dim. Release the idle cut off, then lean forwards and unscrew the kigass primer. First start of the day it needs about eight good shots. Rescrew the primer. Call CLEAR, stick back and held there with your knees and elbow lean over and press the start button. Four blades then boost coil and mags together. Normally she'll go right away and will fire up in a cloud of blue smoke. Immediately check oil pressure and RPM. If its cold allow the motor to stabilise at 700 RPM for few seconds before gently increasing power to 1000 to warm up. On summers day you need to think about moving toward the take off point quite quickly and if you are at an airfield that is unfamiliar with Spitfire operations it is good idea to warn them beforehand that once you've started you've got to go within 5 or 6 minutes. Taxi then. Park brake off, stick hard back, power gently up to 1200-1300 RPM and we're off Slightly over eager application of the brakes and the tail lightens.

Taxying takes a little getting used to but once mastered is very natural and

Continued on P54

Michael Shreeve details the history of Spitfire XVI serial TB863 and its rebuild at Duxford at the hands of the *Fighter Collection's Dave Lees*

Dave Lees working on the Spitfire XVI serial TB863 at the start of the rebuild project. Dave has built many Spitfires and no doubt will build many more.(Michael Shreeve)

During the course of 1944, production of the Spitfire IX was in full swing at Castle Bromwich. The Mk. IX was basically a Mk. V airframe fitted with the two stage, two speed supercharged Merlin 60 series engine. Originally intended as a stop gap until the Mk. VIII with its strengthened fuselage and retractable tailwheel, achieved full production status (the Mk IX in fact had a production run which exceeded its intended production replacement - 5665 being produced, compared with 1658 Mk. VIIIs).

With combat reports showing increasing evidence of operations taking place at low altitude many Mk. IXs were built as LF variants, fitted with the Merlin 66 with a cropped supercharger impeller which produced its maximum output at reduced altitude, compared with the 61.

At the same time licence production of the Merlin engine was under way across the Atlantic. The Packard Motor Company were building Merlins - initially fitted to Kittyhawks, Lancasters and Canadian built Hurricanes, the Merlin in its 60 series form was adopted for fitment into the hitherto uninspiring North American Mustang, producing the outstanding long range escort fighter of the war. In mid 1944, examples of the Packard built Merlin 66, given the designation Merlin 266 reached Britain and it was decided to fit these to the Spitfire IX airframes being produced at Castle Bromwich. Due to minor detail changes for the Packard engine installation a new designation, Spitfire XVI was given to these aircraft, mainly as an aid to spares procurement by units.

The first aircraft were produced in the late Summer of 1944 and were visually identical to the Mk. IXs of the same era, having broad chord rudders and clipped wingtips. In February 1945, production was switched to the low-backed fuselage with bubble canopy, but still under the designation Spitfire XVI. By the time production ceased in July 1945, a total of 1054 Spitfire XVIs had been built, all at Castle Bromwich.

In late February 1945 a high backed Mk XVI serial TB863 was delivered to No. 19MU at St. Athan. It is this aircraft which is now flying with Tim Wallis at Wanaka in New Zealand.

On 7th March 1945, TB863 was transferred to Dunsfold and was then issued (on 24th March) to 453 Squadron, an Australian squadron based at RAF Matlaske in Norfolk where it was coded FU-P. On that date, armed with a 500lb bomb under the fuselage and 2 x 250lb bombs under the wings TB863 flew an armed reconnaissance mission against railway targets in Holland with Flt. Lt. Clemesha at the controls. Later the same day a mission was flown by the aircraft against a similar target with a landing at Ursel (B.67) in Belgium; here the aircraft refuelled and rearmed. Another mission was then flown against the same target, followed by a landing back at the Norfolk base of Matlaske. An eventful first day in service!

After further missions on the 25th and 27th March between spells of bad weather, another recce mission was flown by TB863 on 30th March, once more against Holland based targets. Further similar missions were undertaken on 31st March and 3rd April, before the squadron moved to RAF Lympne on 6th April, flying its next mission, a Lancaster bomber escort against Baireuth on the afternoon of 11th April which included TB863. Another bomber escort was flown on 2nd April by TB863 escorting Lancasters and Halifaxes bombing the seaplane base at B.86 at Helmond and returning to Lympne the following day.

On May 2nd, the squadron moved to RAF Hawkinge and the following day, twelve aircraft from 453 Squadron, including TB863, flew an escort mission to Holland. This time it was of a very different nature - escorting an RAF Dakota carrying Queen Wilhelmina and other members of the Dutch Royal family back to Holland after their enforced exile due to Nazi occupation.

After VE day on 8th May, one further sortie was flown by TB863 on 12th May, covering troop landings on Jersey and Guernsey. After a move to Lasham on 14th June, 453 Squadron re-equipped with Griffon engined Mk XIV Spitfires and TB863 was allocated to 183 (Gold Coast) Squadron on 21st June. The Squadron was equipped with Spitfire Mk IXs, replacing Typhoons at this time and it is unlikely that TB863 ever actively served with them, being allocated to 567 Squadron at RAF Hawkinge on 5th July, allocated the codes 14-E and carrying a red spinner, denoting its attachment to

KIWI SIXTEEN

This page: Two shots of G-CDAN on rebuild at Duxford. Left shot shows the removal of a fuselage skin (Michael Shreeve)

'B' Flight. It served with them in an AAC role until their disbandment in June 1946 when it was passed to 691 Squadron at RAF Chivenor, wearing the Squadron code of '5S'. 691 was renumbered 17 Squadron on 11th February 1949 and TB863 was then re-coded UT-D.

In June and July 1950, eight Spitfires from 17 Squadron were repainted in a representation of yellow nosed Bf109 colours for a part in the re-enactment of the Amiens Prison raid held at the SBAC show at Farnborough. Photographs were taken by the late Charles E. Brown of the Spitfire formation in these colours, together with TB863 wearing its codes of UT-D together with full Luftwaffe markings. 17 Squadron handed over its duties to No. 3 Civilian Anti Aircraft Cooperation Unit (CAACU) at Exeter in March 1951, TB863 being sprayed silver and given a single code letter in black.

However, on 17th July 1951, TB863 suffered an engine failure on take off, resulting in a wheels up landing and damage which caused the aircraft to be struck off charge on 28th September. In 1953 TB863 was sold to the film company Metro-Goldwyn Meyer, and is believed to have been used for cockpit shots at pinewood Studios during the making of the film *Reach for the Sky* during 1955. After this the aircraft was placed in storage at Pinewood until 1967 when it again emerged for potential use in *The Battle of Britain*. However, by this time the airframe had lost its engine and much of the internal cockpit structure and so was moved to RAF Henlow as a spares source for other Spitfires used during the filming in 1968.

After filming was complete at the end of 1968 the aircraft passed into the ownership of Bill Francis and was moved to Southend where it was stored at Francis' home until 1972 when it was moved to the newly opened *Historic Aircraft Museum* at Southend Airport. From there it spent some time at Duxford from 1974 until 1977 when it was placed in storage at Southam in Warwickshire until October 1982 when it was moved to Booker. TB863 was placed on the UK Civil Register as G-CDAN in November the same year, registered to Bill Francis and John Parks. Work commenced on the wings under the auspices of *Personal Plane Services* at Booker before ownership of the aircraft passed to Stephen Grey.

In October 1985 the aircraft was moved to Duxford, home of *The Fighter*

Collection where restoration work began in earnest at the hands of Dave Lees. Once in the workshop the fuselage was stripped of all remaining internal components. All external skins were removed one at a time so as not to distort the structure and used as patterns for replacement skins. The internal structure was found to be generally in good condition and was stripped and repainted before the new skins were fitted. The firewall was rebuilt using stainless steel in place of the asbestos used on the original and was re-fitted to the fuselage. At this time, both tailplanes were dismantled, stripped of paint, inspected and re-assembled with new skins were necessary. Following this a move was made to a new, larger workshop at Duxford where the rear fuselage/ tailfin section was reskinned and the fuselage fitted out. Internal hydraulic and pneumatic pipework was replaced and internal cockpit fittings installed, with the interior being painted in the correct shade of green.

Re-wiring was then commenced, replacing the original 12 volt system with a 24 volt system for ease of operation under modern day conditions, and a luggage compartment was made up in the fuselage behind the cockpit, with access via the radio door on the port side. A tray for the battery was manufactured and installed in the rear fuselage. The centre section spar had new stainless steel web plates fitted and two of the four stub spars were replaced. The

CONTINUED ON PAGE 42

Spitfire LF IXc serial MK912, late of the Belgian Air Force at Saffraanberg, exchanged in 1988 with a Skysport Bristol Fighter replica. The Spitfire is stored by Hull Aero awaiting its turn in the rebuilding shops *(John H. Trant)*

Following a spell away from aviation, a chance meeting with the late Nick Grace brought about an interesting offer. "How would you like to rebuild a Spitfire for me?" Ralph needed no second thoughts, but where should he start this mammoth task? As luck would have it, Norfolk again came into the Hull family life, with an offer to take over the empty workshops at the back of Ludham's blister hangar. Ralph looked over the semi-derelict shops with holes in the roof and walls where the winter gales were to prove as cold as some of the conditions he had experienced in Canada.

The Spitfire fuselage delivered by Nick Grace and the tools unpacked soon saw Ralph surveying the work to be done to bring this low-back Mark XVIII into a high-backed Mark XIV configuration as a static display airframe. The aircraft, one of a number brought into the UK by the late Ormond Haydon Baillie, had changed hands a number of times, had lost its wings, cowlings and many other useful parts to different restoration projects and did indeed look in a very sorry state.

Ralph's brief from Nick Grace was to rebuild the fuselage, manufacture new engine bearers, rudder, elevators, not to mention the hundreds of smaller items and fittings. At this time with the *Hull Aero* notice proudly hung outside the workshops, Ralph set to work on this monumental task all on his own. That is apart from all the times his wife Laura was called upon to help with fuselage skin riveting, this in itself a large task considering the fuselage layout changes required by Nick Grace's brief.

Throughout the long cold and dark winters of the first year Ralph and Laura worked on the hybrid Spitfire until at long last the fuselage skinning was completed and Laura could return to family matters and their young daughter. The idea was for the aircraft to be returned to static exhibition standard and subsequent exchange for the Spitfire PR Mk 11 (PL965) of the Netherlands National War and Resistance Museum at Overloon.

The *Hull Aero* part of the project was to rebuild the Spitfire fuselage to resemble a Mk. XIV, for it was this particular variant that that had played such a large part in the liberation of the Overloon area of Holland, with the Museum feeling that a photo-recce version of the Spitfire was a little out of place, it not even having served with the Dutch Air Force except

as a training aid.

The Spitfire XIV/XVIII is one with much mystery surrounding it, for even to this day the true RAF serial number has not been found either on the airframe or in research through records, so if any airframe was to be bastardized then HS649 (as it was known in the Indian Air Force) would be a good candidate. As mentioned earlier the 'e' type wings where sold on early in its life back in the UK and now form a part of the package of Spitfire XIV serial RM927 having been sold to Larry Matt of Chicago. To complete the composite aircraft, Nick Grace acquired a couple of scrap wings, one coming from South Africa (being left over from the Larry Barnett rebuild of his Spitfire IX MA793, "PT672", these having been rebuilt by Nick's own engineers at his Sussex facility) - the second wing was from a Mk IX Spitfire which were discovered in the mid 1960s at the Royal Aircraft Establishment Farnborough, later passing to John Lowe and Larry Matt in Illinois.

With the fuselage complete, Ralph turned his attention to the engine bearers which he had to construct from scratch, using original Supermarine drawings. As this aircraft was destined to be 'ground-bound', Ralph was able to use non-released materials for the engine bearers, but the rest of the work was done as if the aircraft was to fly again. Some day perhaps - time will tell.

Whilst the Spitfire Hybrid project was in hand Ralph was approached by the *Historic Aircraft Corporation* of Jersey to see if he would be interested in rebuilding to airworthy condition one of the ex Israeli Spitfires rescued by Robs Lamplough in the early 1970s. With the Griffon engined Spitfire nearly finished Ralph was pleased to have another project to move on to and soon Spitfire LF IXe TE566 was on its way to Ludham.

TE566 started life, as did so many thousands of other Spitfires, in the massive Castle Bromwich Aircraft factory in Birmingham, it having been delivered to the RAF in early 1945, later to be issued to No. 312 (Czech) Squadron of

The aircraft required a complete rebuild and re-skin, with the wings needing the most attention, and the tail section also required major detailed reconstruction. The 'kit of parts' was far from complete and over the years Ralph and his right hand man, Jeremy Moore, had to manufacture many items, with others coming from Steve Vizard's *Airframe Assemblies* and *Microscan Engineering* where Martin Edwards, Glenn Richardson and team have been most helpful to the project.

As TE566 was to fly again, Ralph was concious that the airframe had to be 100% and therefore jigs for the fuselage, tail section and wings were manufactured, before any detailed assembly could commence.

spent on identification before the long reconstruction process could begin.

With a wing jig constructed in the Ludham workshops Ralph could begin reconstruction work. However it was at this time that an interesting discovery was made; in that although built with 'e' type wings, TE566 now had the 'c' type or at least was found on later detailed examination it was the leading edge wing skins that had become changed. Some time later it was noted that Spitfire MJ730/G-BLAS, on rebuild with Trent Aero at East Midlands airport which

Spitfire F XIV serial RN201/SG-31 being removed from its display position at Beauvechain, Belgium, May 1990 prior to airlifting and delivery for storage at Ludham (Ralph Hull)

the RAF. With the war in Europe over, the Czech squadrons returned to their homeland along with their aircraft. TE566 passing through Lyneham and Manston in August on the flight to Eastern Europe.

Flown in Czech service coded DU-A, TE566 remained there until 1949 when it was sold to Israel, along with many other similar aircraft, becoming IAF2032. Service with the IAF/DF followed until it was phased out and presented to a kibbutz at Alonhim as a childrens playground toy! Brought back to the UK by Robs Lamplough in 1976 TE566 was stored at a number of locations, with limited work being undertaken on it, prior to transportation to *Hull Aero*.

If TE566 is a delight to see, then the standard of craftsmanship on such parts as the jigs and smaller fittings can only be described as one hundred percent, with nothing left to chance. Having rebuilt one Spitfire fuselage, Ralph and Jeremy found TE566's much easier and this was soon completed and stored, allowing their attention to be turned to the tail section. Prior to Ralph getting the aircraft at Ludham this component had been damaged and it needed a complete strip down, with the manufacture of new parts before final assembly could take place. By far the most complicated part of the project was the wings, for TE566's were delivered to Ralph as an incomplete pile of parts. Many long hours had to be

should have had 'c' type wings was flying with a type 'e' wing. The mystery was soon solved, for Robert Lamplough had recovered both aircraft from Israel and they had been stored together. and even worked on side by side, hence the exchange.

Ralph had, after 12 months hard work, completed most of the first wing structure and following re-skinning the second wing took its place in the jig. This time many more parts had to be manufactured, before early in 1989 a trial fit of the wings to fuselage could take place.

The engine, a Merlin Mk 68A, had been away for overhaul with *Aviation Jersey*.

In the Spring of 1989 TE566 was moving on apace when the owners asked Ralph Hull if he would dismantle and store another Mk. IX Spitfire, this time from Belgium. MK912, which was exchanged for a Bristol Fighter replica with the Brussels Military Museum, was soon flown into RAF Coltishall aboard a Belgian AF C-130 Hercules, later going into store at the Ludham hangar. Ralph has surveyed this aircraft, which for nearly 30 years was displayed outside the Belgian Air Force Technical School at Saffraanberg coded MN-P and although having a large collection of birds' nests etc. installed is in a restorable condition!

"When will you start on the Belgian Spitfire?" is a question often asked of Ralph as TE566 nears completion. The answer, given in his broad Northern Irish accent is always the same...."let's finish TE566 first then we will consider the next project..."

As if one Belgian Spitfire was not enough at Ludham, the 3rd May 1990 saw yet another aircraft delivered by BAF C-130 to Coltishall, this time in the shape of Mk F. XIVe serial RN201, which

for the best part of 40 years was perched on top of three steel pipes outside the headquarters of No. 1 AWX Wing, Belgian Air Force Beauvechain. RN201, built at the Supermarine factory in Wiltshire served with No. 350 (Belgian)Squadron of the Royal Air Force at Fassborg, before being stored back in the UK, later to be sold to the Belgian Air Force, taking up their markings as SG-31. Following service again with 350 Squadron, this time in national markings with the codes MN-L it passed to No. 3 Squadron as YL-B with whom it suffered a wheels up landing in October 1950. At this time Spitfires were in plentiful supply and low in price at some £250.00 each airworthy. So it was decided not to repair RN201, it being passed to Beauvechain for display purposes, having gained the spurious codes GE-A and serial RM916/SG-3.

Some 40 years and many birds nests later yet another Spitfire returns to its country of birth. RN201, currently in store at Ludham, will await the owners plans for its future; a future rebuild for Hull Aero perhaps? Only time will tell.

With Spitfire TE566 as its major project, *Hull Aero* hope to have the aircraft complete and ready for its first flight from Ludhams runway within the next twelve months, and by then the next project will be underway.

To start with a dismantled airframe, kit of parts or whatever you want to call it, and a few years later be able to stand back and look at a nearly finished aircraft takes many qualities for a small organisation. *Hull Aero* have come a long way since Ralph hung his sign on the windswept Norfolk airfield. Many a long day and hard cold night having past with some frustration and pride, now Ralph can see the end of the project in sight. To the visitor most evident is the extremely high standard of workmanship and attention to detail of *Hull Aero* on these aircraft, for as Ralph points out " I want to know that this Spitfire will be flying in a hundred years from now..........and for that to happen it's got to be right - there are no short cuts if you want a good aeroplane in the end".

WW Graham Trant

of the four stub spars were replaced. The aircraft was then moved into Duxford's T2 hangar for completion of the rebuild and final assembly.

Work was carried out on the wings, whose original spars were found to be in excellent condition when x-rayed prior to being worked on at Booker. Fuel tanks were installed in the gun bays to give increased range and the rudder and elevator were inspected, repaired where necessary and re-covered with fabric. With parts gathered from many sources and remanufactured by specialist suppliers, TB863 was looking like a complete aircraft again by the end of 1987. The wings were re-attached and a refurbished set of engine bearers, with some new parts, was fitted. Undercarriage legs were installed, fuel tanks (which had been rebuilt and pressure tested in the workshop by Dave Lees) were fitted and systems connected up. A new set of wingtips, of the traditional elliptical Spitfire shape were built, and the wiring was completed. Cowl rails were built and new cowlings made to shape and installed.

The engine was installed in December 1987; a Hovey Machine Products prepared Merlin 266. Detail work was completed to a very high standard during the first half of 1988, and the aircraft was ready for ground running in July with a zero time rotol propeller unit installed. After the successful completion of ground runs a permit to test was issued and the aircraft test flown in September. A total of around 11 hours test flying was conducted by Fighter Collection Chief Pilot Hoof Proudfoot and by Stephen Grey and a permit to fly issued before the aircraft was dismantled and crated for shipment to its new owner, Tim Wallis, in October.

The aircraft arrived in New Zealand in time for Christmas 1988, a culmination of four years of dedication and hard work by many individuals at Duxford, notably Dave Lees. The worlds population of airworthy Spitfires had increased by one as had the number of countries now boasting an example of probably the most famous fighter aircraft ever, in flying order. An especially significant event in view of the many New Zealanders who flew Spitfires in the RAF during the war and a fitting tribute to those who gave their lives so far away from home. WW MIchael Shreeve.

The Author would like to thank Keith Hiscock for providing much of the historical information on TB863 used in this article.

KIWI SIXTEEN: The Sequel

Proud owner Tim Wallis at the helm of TB863

Following the accident to TB863 on 29th January 1989 we undertook to do the salvage on the airframe ourselves. Offers of help came from several companies and the Air Force but as we had just put the aircraft back together following shipment from the UK and subsequent assembly for flight we knew the aircraft intimately. Very often, despite people's best intentions, aircraft often suffer as much damage in salvage as they do in the actual accident.

With the help of Marnix Pyle, Kevin Harris and another helper we disassembled the aircraft at the accident site, camping there to discourage souvenir hunters. We had the use of workshops adjacent to the crash-site at the town of Waipukurau, and we assembled trucking cradles, and trestles and frames to hold the aircraft as we dismantled it. The accident had occured

Ray Mulqueen takes up the story of TB863 following an accident in New Zealand in January 1989

on the Sunday; we had the aircraft dismantled and loaded aboard the truck by the following rainy Friday and, the following day we made the 24 hour road/ferry journey back to Tim Wallis base at Wanaka on the South Island.

Once back at Wanaka we continued to disassemble the Spitfire, but only enough to enable us to make an accurate assessment of the damage. Primarily this involved removing the radiators. One of the undercarriage legs had been torn out during the crash and the other was almost in the same state. The engine was removed from the airframe and we removed a few panels from the airframe and the wings to determine the severity of the damage.

By this stage it was obvious that whilst damage appeared quite light at the accident scene as the aircraft was further dismantled the severity became more apparent; it was now obvious we had a major rebuild on our hands.

The next question was who rebuild the damaged aircraft? We could have done it ourselves and would have prefered to. However, we would have only been able to claim actual time and materials used if we had undertaken the rebuild, whereas a commercial company would charge at the commercial rate. Additionally, had we done the job ourselves we would have had to contract work out, simply not having the time to o everything ourselves. Thus we would e paying commercial rates ourselves! In ew Zealand we are primarily an merican orientated aviation industry; ery few workshops in New Zealand have ny British hardware, rivets, tooling, panners etc. Virtually the only New ealand based company that specialises British aircraft is *Safe Air*, a very large, mi government owned company. They nd to specialise in military contract ork on Skyhawks, Strikemasters, ndovers, propeller work and major odification type contracts. They have a rge, world class propeller overhaul cility and do a lot of work throughout e south Pacific and even further afield. hey have separate avionics shops, ectrics shops, hydraulic shops and are owty agents. We looked at the lvantages and disadvantages of using fe Air for the rebuild of TB863 and it as felt by both the insurance assessors nd ourselves that *Safe Air* should be pproached. They had already shown an terest.

Safe Air despatched their workshop pervisor, Rick Schuyl, to Wanaka to amine the aircraft. This was the first pitfire Rick had seen. We spent some ne with him, taking him through the rframe and highlighting the damaged eas and told him what we knew about e availability of spares etc., and basically ow we could assist them in the rebuild. e damage as such on the Spitfire was sically what you would expect from a avy downward sink rate accident and e aircraft had landed very heavily on its ose with resultant spinner damage ropeller destroyed), engine mount mage, oil tank, lower cowl, air intake sembly totally destroyed, one ndercarriage leg torn out, the other nost torn out, with resultant damage to e scoop radiator fairing, radiator mount ucture. The one that had come out had ne right through the wing and back rough the rear wing spar, damaging the p on the way through. There were ite large holes punched in the top of e wings in the undercarriage area.

The fuselage had suffered quite major mage; its back was almost broken as e inertia had caused the lower ngerons to collapse just aft of frame 11. e skins were severely distorted and ickled on the belly and sideskins ound the cockpit area. The webbing at me 5, between the spar booms was verely distorted and cracked and we re very alarmed when considering the tential damage to the main wing spars. e tail area was undamaged, but the seat s broken, and the throttle was broken. th these were broken by the pilot Tim allis who stepped out of the aircraft iscathed apart from very light bruising used by the shoulder harness.

Armed with this information Rick huyl returned to *Safe Air* to report to

management and I departed for Australia for a few days to research availability of parts over there. I met several contacts there that could assist us. In the event they procured one undercarriage leg, one new section for the engine mount, and an oil tank suitable to make patterns

from for the new unit.

TB863 was then trucked to *Safe Air* at Blenheim so they could de-rivet as required to make a final full assessment of the damage. It was impossible to do this without doing disassembly of the structures.

I visited *Safe Air* during this time and then went overseas, to Canada - along with some deer Tim Wallis was exporting as one of the attendants. So I had a rather unusual trip out there crawling and kneeling along cages full of deer! Following a stay in Toronto I carried on through to the UK where I spent a week with Peter Rushen and Stephen Grey. During this time I visited *Trent Aero* and Dick Melton, and generally telephoned around to see what was available. I was going to visit Hendon and see what was available in the way of drawings, but after discussions with Peter Rushen and Dick Melton and discovering the complications associated with retrieving such material from the RAF Museum when you do not know exactly what you want and how the system works I came back empty handed and felt it was better to pay people who had the knowledge already.

Upon my return to New Zealand, *Safe Air* were waiting for me as they had found it very difficult to do any form of costing. They had done an assessment but until they knew the options involved and had discussed various repair schemes with me it was impossible for them to arrive at a realistic figure. Additionally they needed to know what was available from overseas in the way of

Stephen Grey at the controls of TB863 following rebuild (Ray Mulqueen)

parts etc. to complete the job. So I sat down with them and Rick Schuyl and I went through the job the best we could, bearing in mind neither of us had ever done a full repair job on a Spitfire before. My only experience was of maintaining a Spitfire in Australia and assembling TB863 when it arrived from the UK. So our task was to come up with a fair, logical repair programme and costing to be passed on to the underwriters who obviously needed some accurate form of a ballpark figure prior to proceeding.

It was decided that *Alpinedeer Group* would be responsible, through myself, for the procurement of all spares, components, and liaising and arranging and with overseas agencies for the repair of various components; for example engine mounts, radiators and radiator fairings, plus the engine. I was also to be responsible for procuring and supplying all technical information to *Safe Air*.

The rebuild did not commence until late in June, by which time *Safe Air*'s workshop programme allowed capacity for the job to be taken on and I had procured all the required parts etc. to ensure uninterrupted work there. Additionally we were confident that the back up for the supply of technical information was in place.

Following my stay in the UK I headed back to New Zealand via the USA where I stopped off and talked to John Sandberg and Jack Hovey about the engine, which had previously been rebuilt by Jack Hovey. For one reason or another and due to insurance, logistics of location we decided to let Jack Hovey inspect and repair the engine. The engine was sent here in June for impact inspections and replace/repair the sump etc. as necessary.

The radiator fairings etc, together with all the linkage, the radiator, were all sent to the UK, with Peter Rushen agreeing to oversee all these items. At *Safe Air* the repairs were also proceeding with as many as nine technicians working on the aircraft at one time doing repairs to the wings. Here they had to manufacture a lot of new frames and ribs around the undercarriage and radiator fairing area and on a lot of occasions only had damaged components as patterns. They made an excellent job of it. The pitot head had punched a hole through the left wing and this was repaired which was quite an involved job.

Reskinning the wings on the lower surface around the undercarriage bay area was also quite a task as there was substantial distortion and a lot of areas were subject to disassembly and parts remanufactured. Frame five was pulled right out of the fuselage and was remanufactured using the existing spar booms and some of the original parts but it had suffered quite an impact and distortion.

CONTINUED ON PAGE 45 43

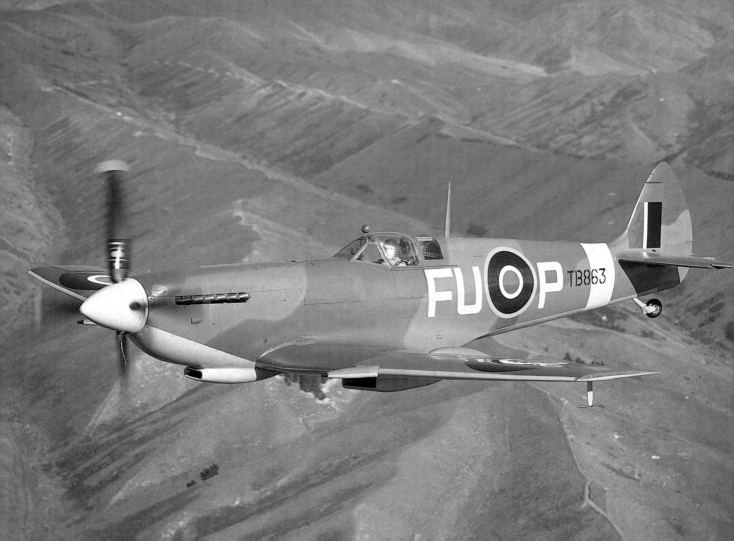

Throughout all this *Safe Air* employed a very strict quality assurance system in their workshop and whereas most restoration shops would just tend to go in and fix something, logically in accordance with normal repair scheme data, AC 43 or whatever you want to use, *Safe Air* could not proceed under this system until they had correct paperwork. And so we were getting more and more of the original drawings sent out from England and at times the job almost stagnated because of this. This was all done to ensure we would receive an excellent product and so we felt quite at ease to go along with this policy, despite the fact it is not what we have been used to with general restoration work.

Meanwhile the hydraulics, undercarriage legs etc, were in the hydraulics shop being repaired or being pulled apart to repair damage - the actual undercarriage legs were destroyed and the wheels smashed. We were frustrated to find that the undercarriage replacements from Australia were too severely corroded to use. So the initial plan was to use parts from the Australian components to effect the best possible repairs to the damaged units. We were well on the way to effecting these repairs, when, by sheer chance, we located two Spitfire legs just three miles from *Safe Air* in Blenheim! A collector had had these together with many other parts which he had been sat on for many years. Bearing in mind we had never had Spitfires in New Zealand, and not too sure what type they were I rushed around only to find there were exactly the same part numbers the ones we had removed from TB863!

At all times on my visits to England and Australia I had been trying to pick up some of the straight axles to get away from the heat of the camber toed in wheels and the subsequent tyre damage on hard runways. I could not locate any of these straight axles which quite a few people would like. But here, just three miles from where the Spitfire was being repaired were two undercarriage legs, both with straight axles on! So I was ecstatic! I immediately took them to *Safe Air*. Peter Coleman was the collector who owned these and he was most helpful to us throughout the job from this moment on and he is a very knowledgeable person with many contacts and he kept coming up with many parts that kept saving the day. He merely wanted something in exchange at the end of the job but not for aircraft use. We were most happy to accommodate him.

In November we seemed to be within striking distance of completing the project. It was at this time that *Safe Air* found that the propeller hub, which had

been pulled apart ready for assembly with the new blades (from Hoffmans in Germany) had a crack in it. Whilst damage to the the wooden blades, which could be replaced, were not looked upon as a disaster a crack in the prop hub was unexpected and this held things up for a while. However we had a brand new hub sent out from the UK - it cost a lot of dollars. I covered the major repairs to frame five, and also the major replacement of the the forward portion of the two aft lower longerons. *Safe Air* manufactured two new sections in accordance with the major repair manual with a slightly modified splice (which I had observed in Dick Melton's shop). They also manufactured new skins. By this stage the major repairs to the airframe were all but complete and we had decided that the wing attachment bolts on the main spars to the fuselage could do with some attention. They were not damaged in the accident but it was felt that this assembly should last for a long long time. As the holes were still a nominal size - from manufacture they had never been increased - and there were some marks in the holes that during the assembly I would have prefered to have attended to at the time. We felt that they were acceptable in the UK and that perhaps we were being too fussy plus we did not have the time on the original assembly due to a very tight schedule of air show commitments. We now decided that we would attend to these holes. We decided to do some progressive reaming, as required, in each hole. This is a time consuming job to be undertaken very carefully. In our workshop at Wanaka we use one of our older, very helpful engineers, Dave Conmee. Dave made, from drawings supplied from England, a beautiful set of new reamers, complete with guides and a reproduction, virtually, of the originals. *Safe Air* then reamed the wing attachment holes and made up new bolts as per Supermarine drawings.

The painter at *Safe Air*, Dave McGill, did a full repaint on the aircraft in accordance with the paint scheme details supplied by Keith Hiscock. A New

Zealand historian, Robert Montgomery, provided some very similar information. So the whole aircraft was painted up in its original colours - those of 453 Squadron; TB863, coded FU-P, as it was during World War II. The airframe was painted prior to assembly. Each wing was painted, the fuselage was painted and then the complete aircraft reassembled during the Christmas period.

The engine arrived back from Jack Hovey in December. It had been in very good condition inside with no catastrophic damage as a result of the accident and Jack had gone right through it and test run it for seven hours - Jack knew the engine would go straight into the machine and we were going virtually straight into airshows. We painted it black - whilst Jack had his own colour - we wanted it to be more authentic. So it was painted black, which caused much comment, for and against, in the large *Safe Air* workshops!

Whilst the engine was being plumbed in and hooked up one of the *Safe Air* Tradesmen became concerned when he noticed a trickle of oil coming from the top of the engine around the coil pump. On closer inspection there was quite a large visible crack in the wheel case the main housing between the supercharger and the engine. *Safe Air* telephoned me very quickly - this was obviously a major disaster. So I quickly made my way to Blenhiem - some 500 miles and about a ten hour trip. As far as *Safe Air* were concerned this was a major disaster; they had been striving to meet the schedule and it had just been blown apart. The crack was discovered in early February. We took the engine out of the airframe. I telephoned Jack Hovey and he was determined that the crack had, in all probability occured during transit. The engine had been trucked extensively in the states, much to my concern, and was freighted out of Vancouver, for a logic I couldn't determine to fit into *Safe Air's* freight programme. It's history now but I feel excess handling had a lot to answer for in terms of the crack. Jack Hovey had obviously done a thorough inspection

Colour Captions Opposite: Top (by Dave Lees) shows Stephen Grey at the controls of G-CDAN during the original test flight programme in the UK. Lower (by W. Ashcroft) shows Tom Middleton at the controls of ZK-XVI taken near Blenheim, 1st June 1990

CONTINUED ON PAGE 48

again. Both Dick and Carol Melton cannot speak highly enough of the true grit and support shown by Mrs. Susanna Church, both to the operation of the aircraft and to the future of the Melton company.

What of the future? Well, it was always Charles Church's intention that some of the Spitfires would be rebuilt and then sold. At the time of writing PL344 was being advertised as being included in the *Sotheby's* sale at Hendon on September 15th 1990.

In the summer of 1990 the Melton workshops are very busy, just having completed a Spitfire fuselage for Australian Peter Crosser (BL628) and work is progressing apace on PL344. Additionally the first *Melton Aviation* Griffon powered Spitfire, an ex Indian Mk XIV serial MV262 is coming along very well. Dick was first associated with this aircraft when it was owned by *Warbirds of Great Britain* at Blackbushe. Rescued by Doug Arnold from a cadet unit in Calcutta, it arrived in the UK without wings, although Charles Church was able to obtain a set in Australia as part of another project. The wings in question had been obtained in Thailand by Australian Peter Sledge and were later rebuilt by *RGC Engineering Limited* at Sandown on the Isle of Wight ready for installation by Dick's engineers. Amidst all this activity the very first Spitfire acquired by Charles Church sits in the back of the hangar much as it did in

1984. "We shall get around to it one day...." says Dick, "....just have to get a couple of other projects completed first" A typical Dick Melton understatement, for this particular Spitfire was obtained by Charles Church as little more than a shell. However it will go through Dick's workshops in due course and emerge to fly from the Hampshire airfield in a year or so.

Although the bulk of current work for *Dick Melton Aviation* is tied up in operating and rebuilding the Church fleet of Warbirds, a new project or two are starting to come to life in the workshops. News of these will be included in future editions of the *Warbirds Worldwide Journal*. Dick has been involved with many other types of warbirds but this is beyond the scope of this article.

With work progressing at a smart pace not only on the rebuild of aircraft but on the many thousands of different parts involved, the workshops of *Dick Melton Aviation* are very well set up for the future, for with the many years of experience of Dick Melton and his team, they are well placed to take on similar work for the future. The business of rebuilding Spitfires can be a tortuous and frustrating exercise which many people across the world have started on with varying degrees of success. However, with Dick Melton there is a man who has taken on the task, undaunted with the trials and tribulations of his trade, and at the end be able to see air under the

Ex Dutch Spitfire IX G-IXCC rebuilt by Dick Melton Aviation, undergoes final fitting out of systems, leading up to a first flight later this year (Graham Trant)

wheels of the aircraft as the subsequen first flights are made. There cannot b many rebuild projects which have no benefitted from the help and advice o Dick Melton seeing them on their way t completion and that much sought afte first flight.

With the care and eye for detai demonstrated by *Dick Melton Aviation* i all their work, there is no wonder tha they give an equal amount of thought t who they allow to fly the Church aircraf during testing and subsequent flights John Lewis, a Rolls-Royce test pilot an display pilot for the *Shuttleworth Trust* ha been involved with Dick for many years flying his rebuilt aircraft. So it will n come as a surprise that John was asked t test fly both Spitfires, the Mustang an Buchon from the Church Collection.

The Hampshire based workshops ar but only a few minutes flight time awa from Boscombe Down, home of th *Aeroplane and Armament Experimenta Establishment* and the *Empire Test Pilo* School. The *ETPS*, renowned worldwid for its exacting standards, is wher Charles Church and Dick Melton hav looked for pilots. Group Captain Re Hallam (an ex Halton apprentice lik Dick Melton) is Chief Pilot althoug these days Reg is desk-bound wit ese days Reg is desk-bound with oD(PE) during the week he is very uch at home in the cockpit of the uchon, Spitfire and Mustang. Under Reg allam's control are Squadron Leader ave Southwood, and Flight Lieutenant ave MacKay, both on the staff of &AEE's Fixed Wing Test Squadron at oscombe Down.

Although their service commitments do allow the three staff pilots time to fly the aircraft on most occasions it does happen that from time to time additional help is required and here the services of Air Vice Marshal John Allison are called upon.

And so, with his long association with many piston engined aircraft and

Spitfires in his blood, Dick agrees that much time will be spent involved with Spitfires and their Merlin and Griffon powerplants, but in time the workshops will see work being undertaken on other types.

Dick and Carol Melton can be contacted on 096 289 685 or Fax: 096 289 691.

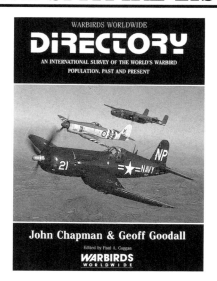

before the engine left California.

After a week and consultation with the insurance assessors we got the go ahead and I started work on the engine. With the approval of the New Zealand CAA *Safe Air* were given special dispensation to do the work under my licence. The engine was torn down to the wheel case area, removed it and despatched it immediately to Jack Hovey who carried out replacement of casings and built up a new wheel case assembly. With all the airlines, paperwork and customs delays we finally received the casing back on 12th March with an air show schedule we could not miss commencing 14th April. So we had an aircraft sitting here, incomplete, engine out, and when the oil tank arrived we found it was the wrong model. As a point of interest the management at *Safe Air* were seriously considering sending the whole engine back to Jack Hovey. I was adamant this would not happen for two reasons. Firstly there was just not the time, and secondly the whole engine would again be exposed to the same ingredient that had caused it damage in the first place - transportation!

With the deadline closing I took one of our men up from Wanaka, Tony Ayers and with the help of one of the tradesmen from *Safe Air* by the name of Murray Cross (who was the guy that discovered the crack) we began re-assembly of the engine. Murray actually offered to give up his three weeks holiday to help ensure the engine was fitted and complete to meet the Warbirds Over Wanaka show date. The next two to three days saw some feverish activity with a great deal being achieved by working late into each evening until finally the engine was reassembled.

Finally the paint was touched up, cam timings adjusted, mag timings adjusted and had it ready to install back into the aircraft. Without further delay the engine was installed by the *Safe Air* engineers. Whilst work had been going on on the cracked wheelcase work on final assembly and rigging of the airframe had continued and detail work was now on its way to completion. Whilst the wheelcase was in the USA the engine was fitted back into TB863 so all the cowlings and front diaphragm could be fitted to the cowl support frames. This also enabled the fabrication, fitting etc. of the air intake system.

The whole project was a team effort, and a much bigger job than ever *Safe Air* had imagined. Meantime the radio man and the electrics team were all preparing their parts for installation. The fuel system in the aircraft, which was an indirect cause of the accident in January 1989, we realised (though pilot error contributed towards it) needed some attention and it was modified to the same specification as the Spitfire PR 19s - an automated system as the air from the vacuum pump exhaust

pressurised the tanks as previous, but as soon as the pilot selects it, there is a float valve in the upper tank and the fuel is transferred whenever the level dropped and stopped transferring if the level rose too quickly. Once the engine starts this looks after itself. So I was incorporating that modification from Dick Melton, which was a complex item requiring a lot of work.

Finally there was an intense period of activity with late night sessions becoming the norm. My wife and family had almost forgotten what I looked like! As the job progressed more toward completion, the more I needed to be there as I was having to certify it.

On 25th March the aircraft was finally ready for its first engine runs. Bearing in mind Stephen Grey was coming out to New Zealand to test fly the aircraft from the UK we had to ensure everything was functional before he left.

The first engine runs were performed at lower power settings and then the engine was stopped and oil and coolant levels checked. Much our total delight the engine burst into action first time. Following the second run I was becoming concerned at the length of time it was taking for the coolant temperature to rise. Suddenly we had a blow off on the main coolant system and of course I immediately shut the engine down. We assumed we had had a major air bubble in the coolant because the engine was running so well. So we let the engine cool and topped up the coolant level. On the next run the same thing happened. So there I sat with the engine not reaching the required temperature when it occured to me what the problem was. I reached for the mixture control to kill the engine and the same thing happened.

After further investigation we discovered we had a shored off drive in the engine, not the pump, but up in the wheelcase. The wheelcase we had just got back from the USA - which we had been waiting for! You can imagine the consternation! Here we go again! After such a worldwide effort, such hard and dedicated work by all concerned it was amazing to find that somehow a 2BA bolt had got into the coolant system! Again, it's history as to how or why but it had ended up in the coolant pump and had managed to jam the impeller and shore up the drive up inside the engine.

After some frantic phone calls and consultations with Jack Hovey we managed to establish that the unit could be repaired without removing the wheelcase or major dismantling of the engine. Jack made some constructive suggestions and left us to it. When I arrived at work the next morning there was Peter Coleman with the replacement shaft and the special tool required, which I had envisaged having to make!

After all the work was complete I

managed to do some more engine runs on April 3rd, and to telephone Stephen Grey and tell him I was happy with the aircraft. Whilst Stephen made his way to New Zealand we managed to do more runs, rectify minor defects, finish small jobs and generally prepare the aircraft for flight testing. April 5th saw us do full power runs on the engine. After more runs Stephen finally ran the aircraft checked everything was to his satisfaction and test flew the aircraft for the first time on 7th April 1990. After a short flight the aircraft was checked over for leaks etc The next test flight was of some 40 to 45 minutes duration and he put the aircraft through a thorough programme. Stephen added this was the first time ever he had been able to put an aircraft through its full test programme on its second flight. So everyone was very very happy. Tim Wallis had meantime been in hospital for surgery and so Stephen and I were very pleased to show Tim a video of the aircraft's first test flight following rebuild The test flight/certification programme was all carried out without a major hitch.

A few days after the test programme the aircraft made its public debut and was seen on national New Zealand television with an impeccable demonstration flight by Stephen Grey.

Late in the day on 12th April Tim Wallis and I flew from Blenheim to Wigram Air Force Base in the Cessna with Stephen in formation with TB863. With just half an hour of daylight left Stephen had a chat with Tim and Tim strapped himself into the Spitfire. With just handful of people in attendance Tim flew the Spitfire doing several beautifully executed circuits and came back and landed with an immense grin on his face and a lot of satisfaction. I really felt for Tim after what had happened, Needless to say this made the airshow!

Tim Wallis and Ray Mulqueen would like to pay tribute to *Safe Air* and all their staff for doing such a tremendous job, Rick Schuyl (who had to leave the day before the test flight), Jack Hovey for his tremendous help, Stephen Grey for his immense faith in leaving before the aircraft was pronounced airworthy and for his very professional attitude and a very big thanks to Peter Rusher Dick Melton, Peter Coleman from New Zealand, Lloyds and our assessor Russell Mason from Needler Heath Kingsnorth in London, the Royal New Zealand Air Force Museum at Wigram and to the often overlooked personnel of the New Zealand Air Transport Division of our Ministry of Transport.

The Blood Red Spitfire

To the purist, Spencer Flack's decision in 1981 to have his newly rebuilt Spitfire XIV painted in the now famous scarlet colours was, to say the least, a radical move! As Spencer was was heard to remark "I like it, and when you have your own Spitfire you can paint it any colour you like!" So the Griffon powered aircraft was soon to become famous as it appeared at airshows all over Europe together with others from the Flack stable - the Sea Fury FB11 G-FURY and the single seat Hunter F.51 G-HUNT.

Like so many people Spencer Flack had often dreamt of owning and flying a Spitfire. Years as a successful Hertfordshire businessman allowed him to eventually to become a part of the warbird scene with the purchase of an ex German target towing Sea Fury G-COW (now flying in Santa Monica, California, as N281L). This was later followed by the single seater Fury, VJ244 soon to become G-FURY. The Flack warbird stable was born but still no Spitfire. However, early in 1979 Spencer noticed an advertisement in *Flight International* offering two Spitfire Tr.9s and the Griffon powered FR.Mk. XIV, then part of the *Strathallan Collection* based in Scotland. The Mark 14 Spitfire

Graham Trant examines the checkered history of Spitfire Mk XIV NH904, perhaps best known for its beautiful scarlet markings.

offered for sale by the Sir William Roberts Collection had a very checkered history prior to its arrival at the small grass airfield in Perthshire, where the Strathallan collection was based on the Roberts family estate. The aircraft that was later to become G-FIRE had started life as part of a contract batch ordered from Vickers Supermarine and built in 1945 at the Aldermaston dispersal factory in rural Berkshire, 50 miles or so west of London.

Built as an FR (Fighter Recce) Mark XIV with an 'e' type wing armament consisting of two 20mm cannons and two .5 inch machine guns and issued with RAF serial number NH904 (Constructors Number 6S648206). The new Spitfire was test flown from the Aldermaston airfield which was later to become the home for the *United Kingdom Atomic Weapons Research Establishment,* and after release delivered to the RAF at Number 6MU, Brize Norton deep in the Oxfordshire

countryside. The Brize Norton unit was one of the major receipt locations for Spitfires from the many production units in England and where aircraft were fitted with operational equipment, armament, radios etc., prior to their issue to front line units. NH904 did not have to remain in readiness at Brize Norton for very long, as it was soon allocated to a Canadian Squadron of the Royal Air Force - 414 Sqn. - making an operational sortie in the hands of Flt. Lt. Woloshuk with enemy contact in the Cloppenburg area on the 13th April 1945.

The next recorded activity was just two days later when Flying Officer W L C Bishop, flying from the Squadron's base at Rheine (B108 landing Ground) in Germany, had trouble with the throttle which would not close and therefore a wheels up landing was made at base, resulting in the usual limited damage to aircraft. At that time the war in Europe was coming to a close and with replacement aircraft readily available NH904 was not repaired on site, but

NH904 still bearing its Belgian Air Force markings as SG-108 when it was sat atop the roof of Oscar Dewachter and Zoon scrapyard at Stene in Belgium in June 1965 (S.N. Simms/Graham Trant Collection)

The Blood Red Spitfire

returned by road and sea to mainland UK for repair.

Air Service Training Limited received NH904 at one of its repair and overhaul facilities though records do not indicate which one. By May 1946 the aircraft was ready to return to RAF charge and yet again Brize Norton was the unit chosen for storage.

With the run down of the Royal Air Force in peacetime there were many Spitfires in storage at Maintenance Units such as Brize Norton; the earlier Merlin engined marks were soon to join the scrap line with others being sold or given (free of charge) to many European Air

The Spitfire suffered a minor accident in May 1948 and along with many other aircraft of its type was declared non-effective stock by the RAF in August 1950 and made available for sale, either as scrap or for overseas disposal.

At that time 'Western Union' funding was made available for purchase of aircraft to build up air force strength in European countries who had little or no airpower, and NH904 was part of a batch of 30 such aircraft allocated to the reformed Belgian Air Force. Vickers Armstrongs (Supermarine) acted as agents for the Western Union in the selection of low houred aircraft, this

pilot training schedules. After a period with this unit, which was also known a 'Flight 600' or Escadron d Remorquage, SG108 was transferred t the Ecole de Chasse or Fighter Pilo Training School where it gained the cod letters IQ-V. Flying until May 1954 when it suffered a Cat 2 accident it wa grounded and finally struck off charge.

At this time the Force Aerienne Belg was receiving more modern jet powere equipment through the MDAP and mos

Spitfire XIVe serial RM694 a Hornchurch. The wings from th aircraft were used in the rebuild o NH904. (G P Trant Collection)

Forces, who at this time were rebuilding their strength following six years of war.

Being a Griffon powered aircraft with low airframe hours, NH904 was kept in store pending further use or potential sale until allocation to No. 610 (Royal Auxiliary Air Force) at Hooton Park in Cheshire, not so many miles from the Industrial cities of Manchester and Liverpool. No. 610 Squadron, like so many others was often refered to as a 'weekend pilot's club', for the majority of its strength was drawn from ex RAF pilots who had returned to civilian life, but still had a yearning to fly. The R.Aux. AF continued in this role until 1957, when, in a period of Defence cuts, all part time units were disbanded.

being just prior to the actual formation of NATO as we know it today.

November 1950 saw the sale details completed and NH904 was overhauled by Vickers prior to delivery to Belgium and issued with the Force Aerienne Belge serial SG-108. This batch of aircraft all carried Vickers Class B test registrations in the range G-15-141 to 170, although which one was carried by NH904 was never recorded.

Arrival in Belgium saw the aircraft allocated to the target towing flight at Koksidje on the coast near to Ostend, where it gained the code letters B2-K in April 1951. The Spitfires of this unit were used to tow aerial targets along the coast as part of the Belgian Air Force's fighter

of the Spitfires were retired, a few bei retained for display. Most however we scrapped. Local scrap merchant Osc Dewachter from Stene purchased number of the scrapped aircraft an transported them to his yard. Included the purchase were Spitfire XIVs RM9 (SG-25) and NH904(SG-108). Osc Dewachter cut off the Spitfires win outboard of the undercart with a blo torch and towed the aircraft on their ow wheels the few miles to his yard in Sten With space at a premium both Spitfir were hoisted up onto the flat roof buildings within the scrap yard, whe for many years they were loc landmarks. Apart from their lack of out wings both Spitfires were in much t

NH904 in external store at Hoylake along with RM694 while the latter's wings undergo local repairs in the workshops of owner Bunny Brooks, spring 1967. **(Graham Trant Collection)**

same condition as when they were purchased with engines, propellers and internal equipment still fitted. However, over the years the ravages of weather took their toll, not to mention the odd knock from the scrap yard cranes.

In the 1950s and 60s the warbird movement as we know it today did not exist in Europe, it only being by sheer luck or the odd wealthy owner that many of the aircraft extant today survived. Survive these two Spitfires did, perched upon the roof surrounded by scrap cars etc. and for the most part forgotten, for the Dewachter family simply had not got round to cutting the aircraft up and though the existence of the aircraft was known to the locals and many enthusiasts in England (the author included who visited them in 1964) the aircraft just sat there until English car dealer Bunny Brooks happened to hear of their existence. Brooks owned various garages and dealerships in and around Hoylake in Cheshire, not many miles from NH904's old RAF base at Hooton Park, had been interested in obtaining a Spitfire for advertisement purposes. With the non-availability of Spitfires in England friend had mentioned the aircraft at scene and a deal was done with the

Dewachter family. For £250 the Spitfire was soon on its way (by sea) to the UK, where Brooks had the old Belgian paint removed and a quick covering of light blue applied to cover up the weather beaten skin.

Although Brooks now had a Spitfire he was far from happy. For his wingless aircraft became a local joke as he searched around for a complete mainplane. At first he drew a blank at every quarter until the Ministry offered another Spitfire (RM694) for sale. For many years this had been a gate guard at the RAF Officer and Aircrew Selection centre at the former Battle of Britain airfield at Hornchurch, just to the East of London.

With the closure of RAF Hornchurch its gate guardian Spitfire was removed by No. 71MU and then used as a spares source for the Griffon powered Spitfires of the RAF's Battle of Britain Memorial Flight. Once the BBMF had removed all the useful items from the Spitfire the remains were transported to 60MU at RAF Dishforth in Yorkshire, where they were offered for sale by tender, the first aircraft of its type to be put up for sale in this way for years. A number of people were interested and bids were submitted, most of which were under £100! Bunny

Brooks astonished the then fledgling preservation movement with a high bid of £250 for the aircraft.

As Brooks had purchased RM694 solely for its wings (which later turned out to be the clipped 'c' type) he soon had these fitted to the fuselage of NH904, with the high backed '694 stored alongside in Hoylake. So, NH904 now had wings, which are fitted to this day. Brooks sold the wingless RM694 to J. D. Kay of Manchester Tankers Limited, it passing through many hands before ending up in store in the United States.

Thus Spitfire XIV NH904, now adorned in a light blue paint scheme and sporting stripped and polished wooden propeller blades, became a well known sight in the Hoylake area. However the novelty soon wore off and with space at a premium due to his garage business Bunny Brooks was keen to hear of the interest being shown in his aircraft by certain RAF engineers at RAF Valley on the nearby Welsh island of Anglesey. Flt.

Lt. Barry Stott, based at the RAF's training base managed to persuade Brooks that the Spitfire could be made airworthy again and 1967 saw the aircraft being unloaded at Valley for surveying and engineering work. The well laid plans of Stott and Brooks were thwarted by the Station Commander at Valley who was perturbed to see the odd coloured Spitfire in pieces all over the floor of one of his hangars. Notice to quit was soon given.

It was during this period that the famous Battle of Britain film was in the planning stages and Group Captain T.G. Hamish Mahaddie entered upon the scene and 904's history. Hamish Mahaddie, well known to regular readers of Warbirds Worldwide, had been retained by the producers of the film to obtain aircraft for the epic, then planned to start in the summer of 1967 and his offer to Brooks to purchase the aircraft came at just the right time. The Station Commander at Valley was pleased to see the back of the aircraft. Barry Stotts feelings went unrecorded but March 1968 saw the aircraft on its way to the film company base in the RAF's hangars at RAF Henlow in Bedfordshire.

It was here that the aircraft was assembled by a team of local air cadets (under the strict supervision of Spitfire Productions Engineers) as a training exercise. It was soon given a detailed survey by John 'Tubby' Simpson,

Managing Director of Simpson's Aeroservices limited of Elstree who had been contracted to build up the "Mahaddie Air Force". At first sight the aircraft looked in reasonable condition but the blue paint applied by Bunny Brooks hid a series of problems and with time and money in short supply Tubby's report was not good. Compounded by a report from Aviation Jersey on the Griffon 65 engine, the fate of the aircraft was sealed. As a non-flyer it was pushed into the corner of the hangar to gather dust whilst the rest of the film fleet was worked upon. Throughout the filming NH904 remained at Henlow and into 1969, by which time the film company was under notice to quit its rented hangars. With the Spitfire staying at RAF Henlow until August 1971 when Sir William Roberts (who was by then building his Strathallan Collection)heard of the aircraft's availability.

In the early 1970s, Robert's acquired many aircraft for his collection, among them the Hurricane CF-SMI/G-AWLW, now flying with the Canadian Warplane Heritage, Spitfire ML407 (later rebuilt under the auspices of the late Nick Grace) and PV202 also purchased by Grace and later rebuilt by Steve Atkins, the latter being the most recent Spitfire to fly following rebuild at the time of publication. Soon after purchase by Sir William the Spitfire was taken to his

Sussex estate at Flimwell for storage. The fuselage was later shipped to Scotland and put into store with many other of the collection's aircraft. The plans of Sir William with regard to the Spitfire were never quite clear for at this time he also owned the airworthy Spitfire Tr 9 G-AVAV/MJ772, later to fly in the USA as N8R and now part of The Champlin Fighter Museum at Mesa, Arizona.

Throughout its existence the Strathallan Collection had seen many of its aircraft auctioned, but it was to Flight International that Sir William turned to advertise NH904 in 1979. It was here that Spencer Flack came onto the scene. The Flight advertisement offered the two stored Tr 9 airframes for sale, both of which had by then been stored at a number of locations following their service with the Irish Air Corps. However, in the days before Spitfire rebuilding was commonplace, it was the single seat Mk XIV that attracted Spencer's attention. After all, it was a fighter, even if it was incomplete. At that time Spitfires had not been rebuilt from wrecks to fly again, and a Griffon powered airframe was a little different, with only the RAF's BBMF and Rolls-Royce operating the type. A person never

NH904 being loaded at RAF Valley in Wales prior to delivery to Spitfire Productions Limited at Henlow, March 1968

Colour captions opposite : Jeremy Flack (Aviation Photographs International) caught the all red G-FIRE whilst in a much more sombre colour scheme depicts the newly painted N8118J (Philip Wallick)

CONTINUED ON P63

straightforward. Basically if the rudders are neutral and you apply brake pressure you get an equal amount to each wheel. Full rudder one way or the other and you get brake only to that wheel. In actual fact you can taxi the Spitfire just like a biplane, rudder hard over and a slight blast of power will get the nose turning. The view forward is poor even with the seat fully up and the hood open, so it's necessary to weave constantly whilst taxying.

3000 RPM. Counter the swing easily with right rudder and the torque collapsing the port oleo and wing with right aileron. It all happens very quickly. It is literally power, noise, tail up, see where you're going, bounce, bounce, airborne! Sometimes, on wet grass, you can develop a slightly alarming 'skittering' sideways caused by the torque and lack of traction from the wheels. Despite the nose pointing down the strip the aircraft drifts left. It doesn't

2000 feet just 30 seconds after take o Level out and power back to cruis power at +4 (38") and 2000 RPM givir 210 knots. Handling is totally delightfu The elevator and rudder are very ligh the ailerons are heavier but are ver effective at these speeds.

The aeroplane has been described .

Painted in another special film colou scheme for a TV series MH434 see her at North Weald (Richard Paver)

At the hold we're looking for 15 degrees C on the oil and equal or greater than 60 degrees coolant for the run up. Temperatures and pressures O.K. Power up to 0 boost (30" MP) gently and with the control column hard back. The whole aeroplane is now bucking and shaking like a live thing. RPMs 2300. Cycle the prop, revs back down to 1800 then bak up again - twice. Sit and listen to the note - sounds O.K. Throttle now back to 1800 and mag check. About 75-100 a side. Power back to idle 600RPM. Standard pre take-off checks of TTMPFFGGIOHHHC.

Ready to go, out onto the grass runway. Roll straight, power coming up. The noise is fantastic, particularly with the hood open to maximise the excitement - the tail almost comes up on its own in the first 50-100 feet of the take-off roll. Power keeps coming +6, +8, +10 and

matter too much as you are airborne before it becomes too worrying. As soon as you're flying - about 80 knots with no positive rotation required it brakes on-off, change hands on the control column, right to the undercarriage selector. Its across, down, pause, across pause all the way forwards in one movement and hold it there. THUD, THUD. Red Up on the undercarriage indicator. Release the handle and it should pop over into its gate on its own. Temperatures and pressures OK at 90 degrees, 70 degrees and 90psi, reach back and up with the left hand and slide the hood shut in one smooth fluid movement - 145 knots airfield boundary pull up into a hard climbing turn onto the downwind leg. Power back to +7 (44") and 2650 RPM. Coolant temps now back to 85 degrees, manually close the rad flaps. Passing

flying as if its sitting on top of a gia knitting needle. It almost effortless departs from straight and level flight the pilot's command. The controls a such that you can almost feel the a being displaced as you move them Fantastic. For aerobatics you need minimum of 180 knots for loopir manoeuvres using 2700 RPM and +8 +9 (46"-48"MP). Normally for displa flying we look for 210-250 and maximum of +10 (50"). It is qui possible however to fly a gentle vertic show at +6 and 2650. At the high speeds the rate of onset of pitch whe you pull into a vertical manoeuvre can very rapid and its easy to grey out as th 4 to 5Gs comes on very quickly. This really where the Spitfire excels. Once yo are in to any pitching, pulling figure th nose really comes round at a rapid rat

MH434 in action, again for a television series (Mike Shreeve)

In vertical or horizontal turns you can pull hard with carefree handling as the Spitfire will start to talk to you before it stalls in manoeuvre. This shows itself through buffeting in the elevators 10 knots or so above the stall. Just release the back pressure a little so that you can just feel a slight 'nibble' on the stick and you'll be getting your optimum turn rate. Quite a difference from say, a P-51 where the wing will pretty much just let go. Of course you can pull through the buffet in the Spitfire - the result will be a lot of shaking and juddering, the turn rate will drop off automatically; however if you keep the slip needle control the wing will not drop. Another advantage of the Spitfire is that you can maintain a hard level maximum rate turn and still have enough power to go vertical at the end of it. This is definitely not something P-51s or Me109s can do. The 109 will turn well but with the slats out the energy bleeds quickly to 180-200mph, he needs 250 to Cuban or loop. The Spitfire will loop from its best turning speed.

The Spitfire ailerons are good and bad. They are effective below 250 knots but above this speed they start to feel heavier and lose there precision. This of course

is a problem for following other aircraft at high speed. If an aeroplane with good ailerons is fighting a Spitfire a series of rapid reversals or a diving, accelerating rolling departure will throw the Spitfire out to one side. Having said that the clipped wing Spitfires definitely have better aileron control and are faster, lighter and more precise without using much of their pitching ability.

The aeroplane climbs like a lift. MH434 with no armament or armour plate climbs at 4000 feet per minute with +8 and 2700 RPM and it's possible to disengage from a fight with most other types using this tactic. Diving and downhill acceleration however is not one of the aircrafts strong points. As soon as the nose goes down most other World war II Fighters will separate from the Spitfire initially. If you are really determined the Spitfire will eventually catch up - it has a very high mach crit number but it takes a long time. One of the more interesting dogfights I have had with the Spitfire was with Howard Pardue in Stephen Grey's Bearcat. We would get in a hard turning fight which the Spitfire would quite quickly begin to win - each time Howard would disengage vertically up - then

recommit to a head on attack before wrapping into the hard turn and vertical disengage again. I like to think I'd have been better off trading 2 x 20mm cannon and 4 x .303 against 6 x 50 calibres but it certainly wouldn't have been very pleasant!

In the circuit the aeroplane is a delight. Run and break and pitch up to 1500 feet or so downwind. Brakes on-off, pressure good. Speed less than 136 knots, undercarriage handle forwards, pause across, pause all the way back and now hold it there. Clunk clunk, green light into the gate and idle on the window in the undercarriage selector. Mixtures AUTOMATIC, pitch to fully fine, fuel contents check, flaps - radiator flaps to manual open. Hood open and locked. As the trailing edge of the wing passes the end of the runway all the power comes off and the flaps go down. Down is close to 90 degrees; they move very fast and pitch the nose down nicely into the finals turn, speed is 90 or so bleeding to 75 over the hedge. You can side-slip a Spitfire beautifully at 85-90 knots and again the similarity to a biplane is noticeable.

In fact the wing is so efficient that for

Colour Photographs overleaf: Left Hand Page (both John Rigby) depicts MH434 in October 1985 with Mark Hanna at the controls and the aircraft in the colours of 222 Squadron Royal Air Force. Right Hand Page (both by Richard Paver) depicts MH434 painted in brown and green camouflage for the filming of Forgotten Hero, a television series.

the prefered high rate of descent power off curving approach it is necessary to have some side slip in to increase the rate of descent. Definitely not favoured is the long drag it in type of circuit followed by a wheel landing. The Spitfire likes to be three pointed and even in a crosswind I would tend to go for a wing down three pointer. If you're hot though, loo out as the aeroplane just wants to keep flying and if you flare regardless of the feel of the aeroplane you'll end up with a colossal balloon and finish stalled out at 30 feet! With practice however it's feasible to operate the Spitfire safely from a 700-800 metre strip. Once down it is normally not necessary to touch the brakes until the end of the landing roll. Heading corrections can be contained by the rudder. Generally the aeroplane will run straight. If you do need to use brake then you should lead with the rudder and use the brake in short dabs. It is important not to cane the brakes too early in the landing roll as they can fade quickly.

Taxi in and shut down are straightforward although they need to be carried out expeditiously for as soon as you lose the cooling air through the radiators the coolant temperature starts

to increase fast.

To summarise the Spitfire then. Totally delightful, fantastic power to weight, wonderful tight turns, almost viceless, beautiful looking, definitely my favourite World War II fighter. More than these factors though is the sense of history involved. When you are crossing the channel, leaving Dover behind you and starting to see France emerge from the haze then you realise that 47 years ago young men were doing exactly that same thing in far far more serious

MH434 at Duxford in 1985 with R. Hanna at the controls taxiing ready t take off (Richard Paver)

circumstances in THIS very aeroplar That is when the realisation that t aircraft is far more than a collection nuts and bolts that it is in fact a livir working piece of history - almost a sort glorious time machine becomes appare. And that's the real appeal of Spitfires any historic warbird. They've been the they're part of history **WW Mark Hanr**

fuselage is complete.

Aircraft currently being rebuilt are [Spit]fire XVIs RW386 (G-BXVI), TE392, [.] Mk IX BR601, plus Seafire PP972. [D]avid Arnold is responsible for the day [to] day running of *Warbirds of Great [Brit]ain*, with father Doug still playing an [acti]ve part is maintaining the inventory [and] purchasing new airframes. David [rece]ntly told Warbirds Worldwide that it [is W]arbirds of Great Britain's intention to

constantly improve the standard of rebuilds of all their aircraft and take in only good quality machines. The Spitfires currently on rebuild represent a substantial investment in history and no doubt we shall see further acquisitions in due course from the world's premier Spitfire collectors at Warbirds of Great Britain.

Warbirds of Great Britain aircraft can be booked for airshow or film work.

Call David Arnold on 0959 76976

Seafire LFIIIC serial PP972 at Biggin Hill in January 1989. Since this photograph was taken the aircraft has been dismantled and restoration to flying condition has commenced at the hands of two contractors (Top by Paul Coggan) Lower (by Richard Paver) depicts the rare Mk XVIII G-BRAF during final checks before its first flight at Biggin Hill following a period of storage

Bill Greenwood details a step by step guide to the basics of flying the Spitfire from the flight planning stage through to the operating limitations of his two seat Spitfire TR9

Bill Greenwood's beautiful Spitfire IX serial TE308 baking in the sun at Oshkosh in 1988 (Mike Shreeve)

uel and range are vital. Remember the Spitfire is a short range defensive fighter, not a P-51 stang type long range escort plane. Nor is it a general aviation aft burning 10 gallons per hour. At power the Merlin guzzles 150 gallons hour and when it's gone there is no ve to switch to!

My two seat version holds 109 U.S. ns (1.21 per imperial) in four wing s and one fuselage tank. Wing fuel matically feeds the main tank, but e is only one gauge on the main tanks hen your wing tanks are empty the n gauge will begin to drop. At 25 erial gallons you have an equivalent J.S. gallons remaining, that is about ninutes at slow cruise power. This is a fortable safety margin and in six years ying I have only landed three times ng broken into the reserve.

or cross country flying I usually run 0 rpm at 0 or +2lbs boost. This ns 47 to 52 gph and gives a true eed of 210-215 kts. I plan maximum nautical mile legs - the longest leg I have ever flown (internal fuel) is 371 nautical miles with some tailwind. For longer trips I have a 60 U.S. gallon slipper tank (we can make new ones) which adds an hour at a cost of about 10-15 knots of airspeed so I plan 525 nautical mile legs, maximum, plus reserves. Handling is only slightly degraded with some pitch oscillation at low speed when full. We usually run it dry in the air if over decent terrain, to make it easier to carry after removing it for airshows. The engine cuts abruptly but restarts readily without boost pump or prime.

RUNWAY REQUIREMENTS

I prefer 4000 feet length, more if at high altitude like Aspen's 8000 feet elevation. For crosswinds 10 knots is OK, 15 knots if the runway is wide, and at 20 knots I'd elect to go elsewhere. I use 50' as minimum width, and suprisingly more than 100 feet width takes away some of my side perception. I have landed on 2900' at sea level and used about 3/4 of it with moderate braking. The Spitfire handles well on landing but lacks forward visibility on final approach.

WEATHER

I have the original vacuum instruments and they work very well.I could fly IFR but think it is safer to stay in good weather, although I have flown over an overcast. Most accidents seem to have more than one cause, so if I especially try to avoid a situation of bad weather, low fuel and without a suitable runway at hand. I do carry IFR charts as well as sectionals.

PREFLIGHT

In any plane I fuel up after landing so as to avoid the temptation to take off low on fuel. With the Spitfire I usually top up the oil, coolant, hydraulics, portable oxygen and tyres the day before a trip and wash the canopy   Thus, preflight is just check fuel, oil, and a normal walk around inspecting controls, radiators, propeller and strut extension. There is no fuel sump drain. If carrying baggage we put a very small bag in one wing locker, tools in the other and a small bag behind my seat on a shelf. Its certainly no DC-3! Finally arrange the oxygen masks and and make sure the air valve is on. And remember to keep track of time and fuel consumption en route!

For short trips this isn't as neccessary and one can run more power and fly it like a fighter at 2400rpm, +4 lbs boost yields 244kts, 280mph at 80 gallons per hour. *WW Bill Greenwood.*

Oshkosh 88: Hot and dusty - Bi[...] Greenwood in the cockpit of th[...] Spitfire (Mike Shreeve)

PS: If any reader has an original Smith's fully aerobatic attitude indicator (artificial horizon) gyro, I need a couple. Mine looks original, but are not aerobatic. Please contact Warbirds Worldwide and they will forward correspondence.

TE308 basks in the Oshkosh sun. Th[...] heat and the intolerable dust was [...] major problem here in 1988 (Micha[...] Shreeve)

be put off, Spencers' mind was made p - the fighter it had to be and a deal as struck with Sir William Roberts. The ollection of parts and the Griffon engine ere soon on their way to Spencer's angar at Elstree, later to be joined by the ings from the Flimwell farm store in ebruary 1979.

Due to the existing rebuild rebuild rojects on the Hunter and Sea Fury king place at Elstree space was at a remium and the Spitfire was transferred Spencer's home at Shenley, where in he hangar on his small airstrip engineer igel Huxtable started work on the build. A detailed survey took place with he airframe being photographed in detail d in April of that year Les Choles, an RAF Spitfire man joined the team at henley whilst Spencer started to look ound for specialist engineering help. olls-Royce, who by this time had ceased overhaul Griffons commercially were elpful with technical advice but it was to e United States and Sylmar, California sed Dave Zeuschel's Zeuschel Racing ngines that Spencer turned to for help ith the Griffon 65 powerplant. Dave euschel (who was killed in 1986, but euschel Racing Engines is now run by s widow) was well known for his Merlin ngine rebuilds but also had experience Griffons, so he was well placed to ssist with the rebuild. So the tired ooking engine was shipped off to alifornia whilst Spencer and his team oked to other problems confronting the roject.

As this composite aircraft - the fuselage low back NH904 and wings of the igh-backed RM694 had, in respective fferent locations, been subject to the ements for so many years the first task as to X-ray the major stress sensitive eas to check structural integrity. Despite e airframe's appearance, all was well, rticularly in the wing spar area. Whilst ot impossible to replace the wing spars ere at that time a difficult item to urce (the new manufacture process was ot at that time under way). Many areas skin on the fuselage were in need of placement , together with a notorious eak point in the Spitfire - the agnesium alloy rivets, which in rtime manufacturing processes were t designed to last more than a few rs, let alone well over 30! With work the fuselage well under way attention s turned to the wings where all skins d to be replaced, apart from the D box tions on the leading edge which were good shape considering the rough

treatment they had received over the years.

Although Spitfire wings, in particular the Mk. XIV variety are interchangeable between aircraft the size and alignment of the through spar bolt holes between the wing and fuselage spars are critical. As luck would have it those on NH904/RM694 were within limits and after manufacture of new bolt hole reamers the wings were able to be fitted to the almost complete fuselage.

Whilst work had been progressing on the airframe Spencer had turned his attention to the question of the propeller. Whilst a set of five overhauled blades had come with the kit of parts he was missing a hub. However a search in various locations in Belgium did at last turn up a hub of sorts together with some additional spares. The original UK manufacturer, Rotol, now part of the Dowty Rotol Group in Gloucestershire had ceased to be involved with the overhaul of this type of unit Spencer had to turn to the West German company Roder Prazision near Frankfurt. Known for their work on Sea Fury propeller overhaul in the days of the German Target towing Furies and later for the warbird movement, Roder agreed to take on the project despite the fact they had no experience with this type of propeller - and so the collection of parts were soon on their way to Egelsbach.

With the filming of the Battle of Britain under way in 1968 the film company, faced with atrocious weather, and resultant rising costs, decided to take the aerial unit to Montpellier in the South of France to finish off various sequences. A total of nine Spitfires, in company with three Hispano Buchons escorted by the Mitchell camera ship spent three weeks in the French sunshine and completed the necessary filming.

On the day before the aircraft of the film fleet were due to return Northwards to the damp English summer one of the Battle of Britain Memorial Flight's aircraft suffered propeller damage. The PR.19, leased by the Ministry of Defence to Spitfire Productions, was taxiing at Frejorgues Airport, Montpellier, when a stone was thrown up by prop wash, chipping a chunk out of one of the aircraft's propeller blades. As the return flights had all been planned Tubby Simpson of Simpson's Aeroservices decided that the PR.19 could not return with a damaged propeller, so with the rest of the fleet getting airborne Tubby set to work on PM631's propeller blades

with a saw!

The damaged tip needed some 2" sawing off to make it good and the other four good blades soon had the same treatment! After some minor adjustments Tubby was satisfied with the balance and following an air test by its RAF pilot PM631 was ferried back to Duxford in company with A Piper Twin Comanche. However! The Royal Air Force were displeased at having their Spitfire attacked with a saw, despite the fact that this was standard wartime procedure for such slight damage. Following internal consultation the RAF decided that this set of blades should be replaced at the film companies expense!

PM631 returned to the RAF with its new blades and the cropped set formed part of the large spares holding later sold by the film company, which finally passed to Sir William Roberts. It was this set of blades, just two inches too short, that were to form the basis of the Roder overhauled unit.

With progress on the airframe going well the Griffon engine on rebuild in California and the propeller unit in Germany the rebuilding team then had the many systems for fuel, electrics, coolant etc. to obtain, rebuild, manufacture from new before final fitting out and assembly could take place in the Elstree hangar. A windscreen turned up from Australia, canopy from a new mould made in the UK while Spitfire historian Peter Arnold had taken on the job of manufacturing the instrument panels. As this Spitfire was stripped of its armament and Spencer was keen to display the aircraft in Europe, the opportunity was taken to fit tanks in the ammunition bays.

Thus tankage was sufficient with the fuselage tanks, wing leading edge tanks (of 12.5 gallons capacity each) and the newly installed gunbay tanks to preclude use of the rear fuselage tank on the majority of flights. This rear fuselage tank really looked upon by the RAF for ferry flight purposes, has some tight rules governing its operation, not to mention a very awkward filler, and therefore unless the maximum range of over 1000nm was required or it was advantageous to pick up a full load of fuel, the tank was not used.

In the early weeks of 1981 just over two years since Spencer had seen the advertisement for the aircraft in Flight International, the aircraft was assembled at Elstree for the start of systems checks, which once complete allowed the aircraft to undergo a Civil Aviation Authority inspection, although they had been involved in the rebuild from the start. ave Zeuschel arrived from California to carry out final checks on the newly installed Griffon engine and to carry out engine runs in early March.

With the aircraft ready for its first test flight from Elstree's 2100 foot long airstrip Spencer's choice of pilot became known for at that time Ray Hanna had a wide experience of flying the type, albeit on Merlin powered variants. To such an outstanding pilot of course this was not a daunting task.

On the 14th March 1981 Ray Hanna flew the primer painted Spitfire complete with its registration G-FIRE from the runway at Elstree. Staying in the immediate area carried out performance checks before treating Spencer Flack and his restoration team to some low runs across the airfield. A few adjustments were needed to trim following this first flight with Ray making some flights later that same day.

The following day, Spencer's dream came true when at last he was able to strap into the Spitfire and get airborne from Elstree to continue the test schedule prior to the CAA air test being carried out by their test pilot Darrel Stinton. Upon completion of the test schedule the CAA Permit to Fly was duly issued.

Painted up in the Flack scarlet colours complete with white and blue cheat lines the Spitfire attended a number of airshows in the summer of 1981. As part of the restoration high intensity strobe lights were fitted to the cannon points, giving a realistic impression of cannon fire!

Spencer displayed the aircraft at a number of shows, both in the UK and Europe before the Waddington Sea Fury accident which grounded him for a while. Following the accident in the 'Fury, G-FIRE was offered for sale. It was not however until February 1983 that the aircraft was registered to a syndicate trading as Classic Air Displays Limited. During this time G-FIRE spent some time based in Europe between displays also suffering periods of unserviceability with engine problems, not to mention two damaged propellers. One such incident happened at Newtonards in Northern Ireland, requiring Craig Charleston to fly over a dismantled propeller in the back of a Beech King-Air to effect the change.

In the late 1980's G-FIRE managed to put in a number of airshow appearances, one of its last being the special Spitfire gathering at Duxford in July 1988 where it was flown to great effect by Pete Thorn, recently retired from the RAF following a number of years as a pilot with the Battle of Britain Memorial Flight.

Classic Air Displays having decided to part company with the aircraft it found a ready home at Bob Pond's Planes of Fame East Museum based at Minneapolis in the United States though Stephen Grey does maintain an interest in the machine.

Bob felt that the Spitfire should shed its scarlet colours in favour of a more warbird military paint scheme and so G-FIRE (which had become N8118J in the USA) was repainted in camouflage and coded W2-P - used on 80 Squadron Spitfire Mk.24s in Hong Kong in the early 1950s.

Thus, the still famous blood re Spitfire entered another chapter in its very varied and colourful life which started some 45 years ago in the Berkshire countryside. Warbirds Worldwide will no doubt follow the future of this wonderful aeroplane in future editions of the journal.

SPITFIRE

WARBIRDS TODAY